**Straight ~~from~~ ~~the~~ ~~stories~~ ~~of~~ couples
who have su~~ccessfully~~ ~~re~~written the rules,
Stay-at-Home Dads will help you:**

• Choose the lifestyle structure that works for you
—whether you're a couple considering a temporary change
with built-in plans for dad's career reentry
—or a working mom who wants to help her
at-home husband start a part-time business

• Learn why two incomes can sometimes cost you more

• Discover the benefits of "dadcare" versus daycare

. . . and much more.

LIBBY GILL has worked in development, production, and corporate communications for Studios USA, Universal Television, Sony Pictures Entertainment Television Group, and Turner Broadcasting West Coast. During that time, her husband has been a stay-at-home dad to their two young sons. Ms. Gill currently serves on the Board of Directors for Slowlane.com, the definitive online resource guide for stay-at-home dads. She lives with her family in Manhattan Beach, California.

Stay-at-Home

Dads

The Essential Guide to Creating the New Family

LIBBY GILL

A PLUME BOOK

PLUME
Published by the Penguin Group
Penguin Putnam Inc., 375 Hudson Street, New York, New York 10014, U.S.A.
Penguin Books Ltd, 27 Wrights Lane, London W8 5TZ, England
Penguin Books Australia Ltd, Ringwood, Victoria, Australia
Penguin Books Canada Ltd, 10 Alcorn Avenue,Toronto, Ontario, Canada M4V 3B2
Penguin Books (N.Z.) Ltd, 182–190 Wairau Road, Auckland 10, New Zealand

Penguin Books Ltd, Registered Offices: Harmondsworth, Middlesex, England

First published by Plume, a member of Penguin Putnam Inc.

First Printing, September 2001
10 9 8 7 6 5 4 3 2 1

CIP data is available.
ISBN 0-452-28274-8

Printed in the United States of America
Set in Transitional 521 BT
Designed by Eve L. Kirch

*This book is dedicated to
Ned, Harrison, and Zachary,
who have brought more love
and light into my life than
words can ever express.*

Contents

Stay-at-Home Dads

Chapter 1

Who's Minding the Kids?

It's seven o'clock on a Tuesday morning In the Hunter household, mom Nancy sits down to the newspaper and a second cup of coffee while her two daughters eat their breakfast, Blue's Clues playing quietly in the background. Nancy's husband, Eric, takes a long shower and gets ready for a busy day.

Meanwhile next door at the Wilsons' house, parents Elise and Daniel madly stuff backpacks full of snacks and toys, gather up sweatshirts, and herd their two daughters into the car. Elise needs to drop the girls at daycare early so she can make it to the office for an 8:30 meeting. Daniel's promised to duck out of work by six tonight so he can pick them up before the center shuts down for the evening.

S ame family composition, similar income levels; even the floor plans of their ranch homes are nearly identical. So what makes these two families so radically different from one another? The Hunter household has a full-time, stay-at-home parent, while in the Wilson family, both parents work full-time outside the home. But while plenty of families have a full-time parent at home, what makes Eric and Nancy Hunter part of a growing trend is just *who* goes to the office and *who* stays home.

Like approximately 2½ million men across the country, Eric Hunter is a full-time stay-at-home dad, while his wife is the family's primary breadwinner. And just like those other pioneering couples, Nancy and Eric have had to make some compromises to create a one-income, role-reversed family structure that works. But despite Nancy's concern that she is not home enough for her girls and Eric's feeling like an oddity in his own neighborhood, they wouldn't trade their lifestyle for the world.

The Wave of the Future

We've all seen dads like Eric around the neighborhood. The ones who always seems to be . . . well, *around*. Shopping in the frozen foods section of the market with a couple of kids hanging off the back of the grocery cart. Driving carpool home from school in the afternoons. Or just hanging out, shooting hoops with the kids while chatting with the next-door neighbor about summer camps or statewide testing. The mail carrier knows them. So do the UPS lady, the dry cleaner, and the school crossing guard.

You may not have realized it, but these dads are the wave of the future. Sure, they look like regular guys. And in a lot of ways, they are. But they're also pioneers, exploring the frontiers of a family option that's always been there but is now catching on like wildfire.

Not Your Parents' Family

No one knows exactly when or where the stay-at-home-dad (SAHD, for short) movement started. Throughout history, of course, there have always been fathers who have maintained primary or shared parenting responsibilities. In many agrarian cultures, for example, both parents, and often extended-family members like grandparents or aunts and uncles, had joint responsibility for childcare just as they shared upkeep of the farm or family business. But as our society became increasingly industrialized and metropolitan, more men's work began to migrate to factories, shipyards, and offices, leaving women to take the primary, and in some cases, sole, responsibility for childcare.

The biggest gender role shift in recent memory began in the late 1970s. During those uncertain economic times, many working men, possibly the most since the Great Depression, were laid off, scaled back, or otherwise downsized out of their professions. Suddenly, men who had functioned in the traditional breadwinner role for their entire adult lives were face to face with their families—full-time for the first time. Conversely, women were just beginning to reap the hard-won fruits of the women's movement and, despite the fact that they have yet to receive compensation equivalent to that of their male counterparts, they were finding many new occupational avenues open to them. The glass ceiling might not have shattered, but it certainly had a few good cracks in it. Wide enough for women with drive, ambition, and perseverance to wedge their way through, allowing others to follow.

But even as men were suddenly finding their economic options limited in ways they had rarely experienced before, they were also enjoying their first taste of "male liberation," so dubbed as a sort of gender flip-side to the women's movement. Men were finally giving themselves permission to become more actively involved in their family lives than ever before and, to their surprise, were even beginning to get society's approval for it. Just as this philosophical shift allowed men to explore their nurturing, tender side, women were entering the workplace in greater numbers than ever before. And not just as teachers or nurses, often the only career options available to their mothers; they were taking on traditionally male pursuits, becoming attorneys and scientists and construction foremen (okay, forewomen, if you must) and almost anything else they wanted to be.

Some of those displaced dads from the 1970s stayed home and raised their kids as a stopgap measure, desperately hoping to get back to work as soon as possible. Other dads found that they really enjoyed parenting and adapted quite well, overcoming—or at least ignoring—the feeling that they were strangers in a strange land. Most dads found themselves somewhere in between, enjoying the experience of bonding on a deep level with their children, but also wishing that it had been a conscious decision rather than a circumstantial necessity.

This loosening of traditional gender roles not only gave both men and women newfound freedom to explore aspects of their personal and professional lives that had historically been unavailable to them, but also prepared the way for the concept of co-parenting. Co-parenting—defined as parents' sharing, substantially although not necessarily equally, in decision-making and responsibility for the physical and emotional care of their children—is now a primary expectation among engaged and newly married couples. According to a long-term study on the priorities of couples researched by child development expert Joseph Pleck at the University of Illinois, co-parenting climbed from the eleventh-place priority in 1981 to the second-place priority in 1997, a mere sixteen years later.

This newly perceived freedom to redefine gender roles combined with an increased desire that both parents be more fully involved in their children's lives, allowed couples to rewrite if not literally reverse, the rules for Mom and Dad. This subtle but potent paradigm shift led the way for the growing trend toward the stay-at-home dad/working mom (SAHD/WM) family structure profiled in this book. Although the movement is just beginning to reach critical mass and popular acceptance, a profile of the "typical" role-rewriting couple has begun to emerge over the past decade.

Dr. Robert Frank has been a stay-at-home dad, a psychologist, and a professor of psychology at De Paul University and Oakton Community College in suburban Chicago. Dr. Frank recently surveyed stay-at-home fathers through the quarterly newsletter *At-Home Dad*, which you will find listed in the Resource Guide in the back of this book. He compared data from 371 primary caregiving dads (dads who have primary childcare responsibility at least thirty hours per week) of 650 children to 490 women caring for 874 children. The "typical" at-home-dad family is described by Dr. Frank as follows:

> *There are two children who have been at home with their 38-year-old father for at least three years. The parenting arrangement was chosen because the parents did not want to put their children in daycare and because the mother made more money. The mother is "extremely satisfied" with the arrangement, as is the father.*

What began as an economically based shift in traditional career roles for men and women as *individuals* has evolved into a new family dynamic for *couples*. There was suddenly an entirely new structural option—role-reversed parenting—open to both men and women. The problem was, most couples didn't recognize it as an alternative that they could choose for themselves. It was still something you fell into or that happened to you by default, rarely by design.

And that brings us to today. With advanced technologies, home-based businesses, and telecommuting, we have more career and lifestyle options than ever before. We also have longer life spans and greater control over our reproductive lives; among other things, we can postpone children until much later in life than our own parents could. And with seemingly fewer restrictions and biases about the shape of our families (we'll get to that topic a bit later!), the stage is set for parents to explore SAHD/WM parenting as a real, viable, and, most important, *plannable* option.

The Daycare Dilemma

Before we begin to explore how the stay-at-home dad/working mom option can work for you, let's first consider the key question facing today's families who struggle to balance jobs and children: Is daycare an acceptable option? Daycare has certainly been a staple in our lives for the past several decades, and it's become such a common choice for working parents that many don't even ask themselves how they feel about it. They just know it's a necessity, and they do what they must to make the best possible daycare arrangements for their children. Certainly they miss their kids when they drop them off every day, and, of course, they wish they had more time to spend with them, but bills need to be paid and careers need to be advanced. But at what expense?

Most of you are probably reading this book because you have some second thoughts about the quality of daycare. And as you saw from Dr. Frank's SAHD profile above, most couples choose the at-home-dad solution because they don't want their kids in daycare. What do they know that you don't? Before we go any further, let's delve into the daycare dilemma and see what the experts have to say about daycare's pervasiveness and effectiveness. You owe it to your kids.

The Mommy Wars

In the late 1980s, Penn State human development and family studies expert Dr. Jay Belsky announced that, according to his research, more than 20 hours per week of nonmaternal care in the first year of life was associated with increased risks of insecure attachment in infancy and elevated rates of aggression and noncompliance at ages 3 to 8.

He might as well have dropped a bomb on the working mothers of America.

The resultant controversy, dubbed The Mommy Wars by the media, inspired experts, parents, and the press to take a closer look at the data, including the ongoing study conducted by the National Institute of Child Health and Human Development (NICHD), in which Dr. Belsky and other leading researchers participated. The ten-year research project is the most comprehensive study of childcare ever conducted in the United States. According to the NICHD, "the Study of Early Child Care enrolled just over 1,300 children at birth at ten research sites throughout the United States. To date [April 19, 2001], the researchers have followed the children through infancy, toddlerhood, and the preschool years. Children participating in the on-going study were placed in a variety of childcare arrangements, ranging from the most informal (care with relatives) to the most formal (center care)."

The trouble with the research—then and now—is that no one seems to agree on the results or their interpretation. Not the experts, not the media, and certainly not the parents. The early interpretation by Dr. Belsky, now with Birkbeck College in London, seems politically incorrect, even quaint, by today's standards. With few exceptions, our society rarely questions or passes moral judgment on the working parents for whom daycare is an economic necessity, preferring to point out benefits like increased verbal skills instead.

If it's frustrating for the researchers, you can imagine how parents feel when they come to the realization that statistics rarely provide guidance. While the NICHD study seems to prove that children in daycare display better language skills and possess better short-term memory, there is also data that confirms that children in daycare are more aggressive and disobedient, and more fearful and shy, than kids who spend less time in daycare. What's a parent to do?

Two things become abundantly clear. One: you better use your own intuition and common sense to decide if your kids are better off at home or in daycare. And, two: since there will always be families for whom daycare is an economic reality, maybe the point of all these studies should be how to improve that daycare. Noting that three out of five children in this country spend time in daycare, Joan Lombardi, a child and family-policy specialist who once headed the childcare bureau of the U.S. Department of Health and Human Services, summed it up simply, "The country has to pay attention to the quality of care."

Even Dr. Belsky, long blasted by women's groups for his critical stance on daycare, concedes that good daycare isn't necessarily bad. Which is good. Because more children are in daycare than ever before. Ponder these statistics:

- More than half the children in this country are daycare veterans by the time they reach first grade.
- Before they are a year old, 45 percent of these children are in daycare on a regular basis.
- At one year, 80 percent of these children are in daycare at least a few hours a week and a third of them have experienced multiple childcare arrangements.

But finding and affording quality daycare doesn't seem any easier than it used to be. And that's only assuming parents want or need it. According to studies conducted by the Families and Work Institute, two out of three employed parents say they do not have enough time for their children, citing what they themselves call a "time famine."

What Do the New Studies Say?

The brain researchers tell us that caregiving has far more impact on the development of the brain than they ever expected. At birth, an infant already has 100 billion brain cells. What a newborn doesn't have are the networks that connect the cells—the networks that enable, among many other things, thinking and learning. So what is responsible for forming these crucial links in an unfinished mind that matures by the day, by the hour, by the second? The caregiver.

Love and touch stimulate growth. Your smell, your sound, your eyes, even the taste of your skin create the powerful bond between you and your infant and the ways in which he interacts with the world, not only in the moment, but in the future. It's been established by experiment that a stable, secure child produces less cortisol, a stress hormone that kills brain cells and brain cell networks. Emotions and biology *are* connected. Sure, heredity counts, but the daily care of children offers countless opportunities to encourage and strengthen healthy responses.

Where's Dad?

One of the biggest problems with Belsky's research and the current NICHD study is that they concentrate almost exclusively on the mother/child attachment, basically determining that quality mothering + quality childcare = good kid. In the caregiving equation that results in a child's emotional and physical well-being, where's Dad?

Further research shows us that Dad matters and that, in a growing number of caregiving situations, Dad is there. Dr. Kyle D. Pruett, the author of the insightful *Fatherneed*, recalls an instance a mere fifteen years ago when one of his female students, after a lecture about the need for consistent caregiving in the first months of life, asked about the long-term impact of her impending return to her medical practice if her husband were to stay home and care for their child. Pruett, intrigued and dismayed that he did not have the answer to her question, embarked upon a search of the Yale University library system to see if there were any studies about the impact of primary caregiving fathers. In all the library's 12 million volumes, there was nothing on that particular topic. And that's not all.

Pruett goes on to recount that, in spite of the pioneering childcare work of a number of experts in child development, fathers are noticeably missing from the research landscape. He describes a classic critique of this appalling lack: in a leading psychology journal, Vicky Phares of the University of Connecticut reviewed scientific reports on family and child development—and found that fathers were not even mentioned half the time! But fathers were certainly involved in the conception of those children 100 percent of the time. We may have come a long way, Daddy, but we still have a long way to go.

Things are changing, albeit slowly. A 1997 U.S. Census Bureau report, "My Daddy Takes Care of Me," presents impressive graphs and quotes from numerous sources with deceptively dull titles concerning the increasing involvement of fathers in family life. The Census Bureau is hardly known for leading the pack in identifying cutting-edge social change, so if it's on to dramatic shifts in the proportion of fathers caring for their preschoolers, something must really be happening. Statistics vary from year to year according to the health of the economy as well as job availability, but clearly the importance of a father's participation in his infant's care is finally being recognized and acknowledged. Funny how scientific studies often seem to confirm what we parents know already through instinct, experience, and common sense.

Daycare Fear

Even though the hard scientific data about daycare may seem surprisingly rosy, we've all heard the daycare nightmares from the neighbors, in the pickup queue at school, and in the media. Sometimes it's a fairly benign story of a child wandering away from a daycare center and being returned unharmed by a nearby resident. Other times it's a magazine article that lists "Seven Signs for Daycare Beware."

Then there are the less frequent but attention-grabbing horror stories that can shock an entire nation. The incredibly frightening—because they could happen to you—stories of truly evil caregivers caught by "nannycam" on an episode of 20/20 or the nightly news. Or the story of Louise Woodward, the nanny who shook her young charge to death.

But there's another kind of daycare fear far less heinous than those incidents at the extreme end of the scale, but more common. It's the caregivers who don't really care about your kid. Or, at least, not deeply. And why should they? They're not family. They're paid help, hired by the hour or the day or the week to render services. Not to render passion, love, or parental insight, although some may do just that. Sometimes they're almost like members of the family. But are you willing to take the chance that a paid worker could ever parent your child as effectively as you could? No matter how optimistic the research, most involved parents know no one could do the job as well as they could.

Daycare vs. Parentcare

So you've thought about daycare—defined here as nonparental care, inside or outside the home—and now you're thinking about parentcare. Not easy, is it? Not where your kids are concerned. Let's see if this will help clarify things for you a bit. Answer the "Daycare vs. Parentcare" questionnaire, below, to see where you honestly stand when it comes to this crucial choice.

Daycare vs. Parentcare

- When considering the daycare option, are you more influenced by your own feelings or by the opinions of pro-daycare friends and the media?
- Do you think that staying home with your kids is an outdated idea?
- Do you think that young children can be just as happy being cared for during the day by qualified adults as they would be if a parent cared for them?
- Is the fear of either you or your spouse "falling behind" in your career greater than the fear of losing time with your children?
- Do you feel relaxed and happy when you think about your kids spending their day with a daycare worker?
- Do you think that the benefits of a child being around other children in a daycare center outweigh those of being around one's parent?
- Do you think qualified, caring daycare workers can nurture children the way parents do?
- Do you think that children become more disciplined, more verbal, and better equipped to function as part of a group as a result of being in daycare than they do if cared for at home?

- Do you feel that "missing out" on the day-to-day happenings in a child's life by placing them in daycare is simply the price modern couples must pay to provide well for their families?

Did your responses to the questionnaire surprise you? Try running it by your spouse, if you haven't already, and see if you're in sync with each other. Any surprises there? Anything you need to talk through? Whether you're thinking parental care is the way to go or you're still looking for answers, let's take it one step further.

The Dadcare Decision

In Dr. Frank's profile of SAHDs, we saw that in addition to parents' desire to keep their kids out of daycare, the other determining factor was that the wife was making more money than her husband. Most SAHDs profiled in this book say that economics was, indeed, one of several factors in their SAHD/WM decision-making process. Right now, nearly 25 percent of wives in the United States earn more than their husbands. And, as women gain financial parity with men in the workplace, that proportion is expected to grow.

Let's move on to your feeling about dadcare vs. momcare. We'll look at stereotypes—yours and others'—in Chapter 5, and at male and female parenting styles in Chapter 6.

But, for now, let's take a quick survey and see if the SAHD/WM option is right for you. If your family is stress-free, your parental tasks divvied up perfectly, and your careers right on track—and, of course, if your kids are thriving in daycare or with their nanny and blissfully unaware of any struggles you and your spouse might have regarding time, money, or power—perhaps you don't need this book after all. But if, like the rest of us, you struggle with balancing your commitments to work and family, the SAHD option could well be a solution. Whether you have family already or are merely in the planning stages, take a look at the questions listed below and answer as honestly as you can. Don't cheat, now; this is your life we're talking about!

The Dadcare vs. Momcare Questionnaire

- Do you believe that men have the same nurturing capabilities as women?
- Is Dad willing to put his career on hold and stay home with the kids?
- Is Mom willing to accept responsibility for being the family's primary provider and to forgo, or at least postpone, staying home with the kids?
- Do the two of you think you can handle any unflattering stereotypes, ego blows, or other fallout from a different lifestyle choice?
- Are you both willing to negotiate your roles and commit to ongoing communication about your reversal?

If you answered yes to most of the above questions, you are excellent candidates for the SAHD/WM lifestyle.

But let's not stop there. After all, you're making a choice that will affect your entire family, possibly for years to come. Before you make that critical decision, let's take a look at the three most prevalent types of family structures: the traditional Working Dad/Stay-at-Home Mom; the new norm, Two-Career Couple/Kids in Daycare; and the increasingly popular SAHD/WM, which we've just begun to explore.

The Three Basic Structures, or What's Behind Family #1, Family #2, and Family #3?

Working Dad/Stay-at-Home Mom

Joe and Diane have been married for eleven years, ever since they graduated from college together. Diane worked for the first three years, then decided to stay home after their first son, Jonathan, was born. She entertained the possibility that she might go back to work as a bank teller, but once their daughter and a second son were born, Diane decided to shelve her job and become a full-time mother and homemaker. Good thing, since Joe's career as the regional manager of a large manufacturing company was really taking off. The problem was, as Joe climbed the corporate ladder, he fell into the trap that most men of his generation succumbed to: he left home and family to Diane and devoted most of his waking hours to his job. Does that sound familiar? Maybe something like the household you grew up in? Or even like your own marriage and family now?

If so, you're not alone. For years, this has been the standard for the traditional American family. But here's something you may not be aware of: ongoing research, including 1994 and 1996 studies by Dr. Frank, indicate that when Dad works full-time and Mom parents full-time, the kids experience a strong influence from the mother but little influence from their father. Amazingly—listen up, now, this is important—the converse does not seem to be true at all. When Dad is the caregiver and Mom works full-time, the children feel a strong bond with *both* parents. Somehow, despite their careers, the moms in these role-reversed families manage to maintain a much higher level of involvement in their communities, their schools, and most important, their kids' lives. Now, there's a case for role-reversed parenting!

The obvious plus in this traditional type of working dad/stay-at-home mom family structure is, of course, that the kids get a full-time parent at home to nurture and care for them. But although this structure has been the norm in this country and others for centuries, it's no longer as prevalent as you might think. Only 20 percent of two-parent families in the United States conform to this traditional picture of a wage-earning dad, a stay-at-home mom, and one or more kids at home.

Two-Career Couple/Kids in Daycare

Meet Karen and Philip. He's a contractor. She's a nurse. Both of them love their work. Their jobs keep them challenged, energized, and fulfilled. Problem is, they have two small children whom they also love. But Karen and Philip have convinced themselves that they must both have simultaneous, full-time careers in order to be happy and financially fit. What's wrong with this picture? Nothing, if you don't mind placing your children in daycare for up to ten hours a day. Or handing them off to a non–family member to parent. Or even to a family member—just not Mom or Dad.

The two-wage earner couple is one of the fastest-growing family structures in the nation's workforce today! But is it really based on need? We're not talking about single parents or subsistence-level families who need all wage-earners on deck just in order to survive. This choice is made by middle-class (and up!) couples who don't really *need* two incomes to get by. We'll talk about how you can live on one income in Chapter 4, where you'll get some serious assistance with financial planning. For now, let's just say that most of us in the middle class don't realize that we *can* live on one paycheck, if we plan and budget. Not always lavish, but worth the sacrifice to parent your own child. If you're comfortable shelling out lots of money for daycare to continue working and feel confident that you and your child are getting what you need out of this arrangement, then you probably have no problem justifying the "Both Parents Work" option.

Stay-at-Home Dad/Working Mom

Let's go back to Eric and Nancy from the beginning of this chapter. Nancy is the office manager at a car dealership. Eric owned a small hardwood flooring business until their first daughter, Megan, was born. Eric and Nancy knew before their kids were born that they wanted a parent home full-time, although they'd never really taken the conversation much further than that until Nancy found out she was pregnant.

Eric earned slightly more than Nancy, but his work was somewhat seasonal and he carried no health benefits. So they decided that he would temporarily shut down his business, maybe picking up a few side jobs once their little girl was older, then return to full-time work somewhere down the line. "Somewhere down the line" got put on hold once their second daughter, Brittany, came along. By now, however, Eric was a seasoned stay-at-home dad, thoroughly enjoying his role and his closeness with his children. And Nancy, who'd been able to really focus on her career, secure in the knowledge that the kids were in capable parental hands, had gotten a promotion and raise.

Of course, there were trade-offs both Nancy and Eric had to accept. There were times when Nancy's job prevented her from being able to volunteer at school or be home for those little, special moments. And Eric, despite relishing his at-home role, occasionally missed his work, the feeling of camaraderie with his crew and the sheer satisfaction of seeing a job completed. But watching their girls flourish kept them from doubting their choice.

So if you're thinking about jumping off the two-career bandwagon or rewriting traditional parenting roles so you can swap places with your spouse, don't expect role reversal to be the easiest route. It's not. You'll need to do some soul-searching and some challenging homework. But the pay-offs of planning ahead are well worth the investment of time. So open your mind and read on!

Quick Review

After each chapter, we'll recap key points to jumpstart your thinking about parenting options and make it easy for you to review the information presented in this book.

What the women's movement did for men.

Since women began to enter the workforce in record numbers, men's impact on their children has shifted dramatically. Fathers are more actively involved than ever before in their children's lives. Now, approximately 2½ million stay-at-home dads have made it a full-time commitment.

Think about daycare versus parentcare.

While daycare is a great solution for many families, it shouldn't be an automatic assumption. Although the studies about daycare are fairly optimistic, many parents believe that no one can raise their children better than they can. *Who* is raising your children—and *how* effectively they are doing it—may be the most important decision you'll ever make. It's well worth thinking long and hard about, so take the "Daycare vs. Parentcare Questionnaire" to help you clarify your thoughts on this important topic.

What's better for your kids—momcare or dadcare?

If you've decided that you want a full-time parent at home, who should it be? While the more traditional way to go would be for mom to stay home, many couples find that dad is actually the better person for the job. Check out the questionnaire on *Dadcare vs. Momcare* and have your spouse do the same.

Three common family structures.

The three family structures we examined in this chapter are Working Dad/Stay-at-Home Mom; Two-Career Couple/Kids in Daycare; and Stay-at-Home Dad/Working Mom. They are all viable options, but the SAHD/WM isn't always given serious consideration simply because it's the least traditional. But if it could work for your family, isn't it worth taking the time to do your homework?

Chapter 2

Profiles in Parenting

The Top 6 Reasons Dad Stays Home with the Kids

"It's the wave of the future and I'm glad to be at the forefront of it."

—John Lennon on being a househusband
and stay-at-home dad

When John Lennon was staying home with his young son, Sean, today's crop of at-home dads were probably teenagers at home listening to John Lennon. Granted his situation was a little different from most other at-home dads', but Lennon was absolutely right. He really was at the forefront of a movement. And it has grown significantly since he was alive and caring for his son, although maybe not as swiftly as the noted idealist might have imagined.

So just who are today's stay-at-home dads? And why are they home instead of their wives? Are they different from other men, who go to work every day and pick up a paycheck? And what, if anything, do they have in common with the at-home moms who have carried the weight of home and family for generations?

And how about those working wives? Are they shunning their childcare responsibilities in favor of their careers? Or are they honoring their children in a way that is best suited to their natures and, at the same time, most beneficial to the welfare of the family unit? Is this stay-at-home dad/working mom role reversal something that just sort of happens to a couple, or is it a carefully thought-out decision, arrived at only after intense analysis of all the contributing factors?

As will become abundantly clear throughout the course of this book, there's no such thing as an *ideal* couple for the SAHD/WM lifestyle, just like there's no automatic process for adapting to it. There's no *type* of guy who successfully stays home to care for his children. And, believe it or not, no diapering gene and no secret nurturing trait that makes one dad a candidate for at-home daddy-dom and another a reject. And the same goes for the working moms. Like their at-home husbands, they come in all shapes, sizes, and comfort levels when it comes to being their family's primary breadwinner.

Just like their more traditional at-home mom/working dad parenting counterparts, stay-at-home dads and working moms run the gamut of age, ethnicity, life experience, and ability to make a good grilled-cheese sandwich. Some come to their reversed roles by design, others by default. Each has unique circumstances and stories to tell, but they all share one universal theme and one singular passion. The common denominator linking virtually all the parents interviewed for this book, not to mention countless others around the world, is that they love their children enough to provide the best for them. And that means, plain and simple, a full-time at-home parent. In the case of these pioneering parents, that parent just happens to be dad.

Why would they go to such great lengths to create a lifestyle so different from their own upbringing and even from the lives most of their friends and peers lead today? Because for these couples, the welfare of their kids and the quality of their family life comes first, and they are willing to do the planning, face the stereotypes, and tackle whatever else is necessary to safeguard those priorities. For them, this is not just lip service or moral mumbo-jumbo. This choice is a real, livable everyday experience.

These trailblazing dads and moms are also unanimous in their feeling that daycare is not an option. Nor is nanny care or even nonparental family care, at least not as a full-time way of life. Despite the fairly encouraging results of the daycare research described in Chapter 1, all of these parents know instinctively and without a doubt that no one can take better care of their children than a loving, involved, connected, full-time parent. But that's where the similarities among them end. Each family profiled here came to its choices in its own way, found its unique path and forged roles—that is, rewrote traditional roles—through the courage of the parents' convictions and their love of their children.

Choices, Not Sacrifices

Almost to a person, these parents will tell you that they have made a choice, rather than a sacrifice, in designing a life that puts their kids first. They don't call it a sacrifice because to them it's not a hardship; it's a labor of love. Something they value right up there with integrity, the work ethic, and family dinner. But don't think these parents are saints or martyrs. They are the first to admit that their unusual lifestyles are not always easy, that their roles are sometimes confusing, that they sometimes struggle to provide the kind of life to which they believe their children are entitled, even if it means they must sometimes set their own needs aside. And that they wouldn't trade a minute of it!

These SAHD/WMs have made a conscious choice to downsize, prioritize, and restructure so they can live on one income, get off the fast track, and, most definitely, give up keeping up with the Joneses. They've done the hard work, sometimes by sheer trial and error, to figure out how to keep a parent home full-time. And they've all come to the same conclusion: although it might not have been an easy or obvious choice, Dad was definitely the right person for the job.

Why Dad is the best choice varies from family to family. Sometimes it's purely an economic decision; sometimes—often—it's a matter of the heart. Frequently, it's a combination of reasons that dictate that Dad will stay home and Mom will bring home the Easy Mac. But some common themes emerge from the decision-making process.

If you're thinking about role-reversed parenting, you're probably somewhere within one or more of the categories we're about to explore. Maybe you're already living the SAHD/WM life and want to know more. Either way, you will be helped by hearing these couples' stories and seeing that they are just regular people who figured out how to do what they thought was right for their families. They'd be the first to tell you that things aren't always easy.

Like Hogan and Tina, who know all about stretching a teacher's income to cover the cost of three growing boys, including a special-needs son with sky-high medical bills. Or Jim and Leslie, who can tell you how important honest communication is when parents don't see eye to eye on who should be raising their child. These couples will tell how they chose their roles (or, in some cases, how their roles chose them), how they've adjusted to their lifestyles, how happy they are, or how challenging it's been. What they'll all say is that the most important thing is having their kids cared for by a parent. That's the link in all of their stories. The love, the devotion, the choices—the kids. So let's meet the trailblazers and see why dads choose to stay home with their kids.

Reason #1—Dad Is Out of Work

"For men like me who expected to take care of their families, if not make a million dollars by the time they reached age thirty, it's a rude awakening to discover you're a supporting player in your own home."
—Samuel, unemployed sales rep, on becoming a stay-at-home dad

Samuel was thirty-two when he lost his sales job at a fast-paced Silicon Valley technology firm. Like a lot of people in the volatile digital world, Samuel was a victim of the unstable economic environment, and when his company went under, he was unemployed for the first time in his adult life. To complicate things further, Samuel's wife, Jeannie, an apparel designer, was pregnant with their first child.

But they were lucky. For some couples this situation might have spelled financial disaster. However, since Jeannie was bringing in a good salary and had company benefits as well, it seemed like a logical time for Samuel to stay home for a little while and help out with the baby while he pondered his next career move. Two years later, Samuel was still home with their son, Dylan, and Jeannie was long since back at her job.

Samuel and Jeannie fully admit that they didn't really plan their role reversal so much as it sneaked up on them. Neither was a fan of daycare; they'd assumed they would figure out some sort of nanny-cum-grandmother patchwork-quilt childcare arrangement that would be more than acceptable to them. But Jeannie, suffering complications, was confined to bed after Dylan's birth, and Samuel found himself caring for both wife and child.

Most stay-at-home dad/working mom parents say that finances were the major factor, or at least a contribution, in their decision to switch traditional parenting roles. John Lennon's experience notwithstanding, in the early days of the at-home dad movement, financial necessity was almost always the only reason for dads who were disabled or downsized out of their jobs to stay home and care for the kids. Dads who'd lost their earning capability were forced to find an entirely new way to contribute to the well-being of their families and, as a result, often created bonds with their children that far surpassed those of their working dad counterparts.

For many couples today, economics is still the only reason for their stay-at-home dad choice. With women's increased earning power and the greater acceptance of role-reversed parenting, plus new home-based career options that can provide part-time income for full-time caregivers, it makes financial sense to choose the SAHD/WM option. Although many families figure out how to downscale and live comfortably on one salary—more about that in Chapter 4—SAHD/WM parents can be a relatively privileged lot. Their average household income often exceeds the $60,000 national median for families. And they frequently have health benefits through the wife's job.

But as Samuel can tell you, dealing with the financial ramifications of role reversal is just the beginning. As he learned, and as we'll explore throughout this book, most men are socialized to be providers and are given few tools that prepare them for being what Samuel described as a "supporting player." So even after they've accepted that their career and ego needs will be taking a backseat to their family's needs, men are often ill equipped to deal with the emotional issues that accompany the SAHD lifestyle. Stay-at-home dads often experience conflict over relinquishing personal power, loss of control and identity related to not being the primary provider, and the challenges of redefining what is masculine and what is feminine. The conflict may start with finances, but it always ends with feelings. But feelings can change. As Samuel ultimately realized, being a "supporting player" in his family drama, though it took some getting used to, was an incredibly rewarding role.

Reason #2—Mom's Job Has Health Benefits and Dad's Doesn't

> "Working for the school system, we knew every year what my salary was going to be. I had the health benefits. We knew there was going to be a job there. It was the security of it."
> —Tina, on how health benefits played into their SAHD decision

> "If you're a stay-at-home dad, you don't take what people say personally. You just shrug it off and keep doing what you're doing because you love your kids. After a while, people are going to recognize what kind of a commitment you made."
> —Hogan, on dealing with other people's reactions to his being a stay-at-home dad

Tina admits a little wistfully that she would love to stay home full-time. Both she and her husband, Hogan, are passionately involved, loving parents. Both of them say they would have no problem working or staying home. In fact, they agree that having two parents who both work part-time *and* parent part-time would be just about perfect. And they've almost managed to do just that.

Not that it's been easy. But you certainly won't hear them complaining. They feel fortunate that they've been able to arrange their lives around their three boys, Grant, Wesley, and Matthew. It took some extraordinary measures on their parts, but Tina and Hogan are the last ones who would call those changes sacrifices. To them, it's all about making decisions, negotiating along the way, and doing what's best for your kids. Including selling your house and buying down, so that you can afford to live on one income, a teacher's salary at that. And about sharing one car, something that was commonplace not all that long ago, but seems like a strange throwback today.

Tina is a schoolteacher and speech pathologist. She works in a year-round school system in Irvine, California. Hogan used to own his own wallpapering business, but gave it up when their oldest son was two years old, so he could stay home full-time. The primary reason that Tina became the full-time provider was not that she had a burning desire to pursue her career. Although she loves teaching, Tina says that being a full-time parent would be just as satisfying to her. For her and Hogan, it was the fact that Tina had a stable job with excellent health benefits. And since Hogan was self-employed, his business was less predictable and without the kind of medical coverage that Tina's job had to offer. Although Hogan acknowledges that he sometimes misses his work, he has no regrets about his decision to stay home.

Even though Tina and Hogan had about the same income, their health benefits were critical—even more so than to most families, because their middle son, Wesley, is disabled. Tina and Hogan agreed that they would not want any of their kids in daycare, but in Wesley's case it was out of the question. They felt that no one could provide the kind of compassionate, around-the-clock care for Wesley, or for Grant and Matt, that they could. Their desire to keep their kids out of daycare, supported by Tina's tenured teaching position, made Hogan the best man for the at-home job.

Hogan, a self-described extrovert who has easily broken the barricades and joined ranks with the neighborhood's at-home moms, has begun a corporate seminar program he calls "Proud Dads." Hogan's belief is that, even though dads may be proud to be fathers, they don't always know how to show it. Case in point. Hogan tells a story about the time Grant was in kindergarten and made a paper tie, complete with yarn string, for Hogan as a Father's Day present. It looked like . . . well, like a kindergarten kid made it. Even so, Hogan told his son he would wear the tie the very next time he came to pick Grant up from school.

But sometime over the weekend, Hogan's self-consciousness started to get the best of him, and, bit by bit, he began to talk himself out of wearing the tie. By the time Monday morning rolled around, he was fully arguing with himself over whether or not to suffer the embarrassment and just wear the thing, when he decided he was being silly. He put the tie on and went to school, feeling every bit like a circus clown. As Hogan walked in to pick up Grant, moments away from yanking the tie off, what did he see on the playground? Another dad, looking just as silly in *his* paper Father's Day tie. They each smiled, recognizing that they were kindred spirits. That, Hogan explains, is the essence of being a Proud Dad.

Reason #3—Dad Passionately Believes in Being an At-Home Parent

> "I finally just gave my wife an ultimatum and told her, 'One of us needs to stay home.' "
>
> —Jim, on his moral dilemma about daycare

Sometimes economics has little bearing on the stay-at-home dad decision, except for the recognition that there will be some belt-tightening after the decision is made. Sometimes a parent simply can't stand the thought of their child being raised by a non-parent, no matter how good that third-party care might be. These parents know in their hearts and souls that they should be caring for their children, each and every day. Sometimes the parent who reaches that inevitable conclusion is Dad.

Jim and Leslie were both successful in their careers, although Leslie was by far the bigger wage-earner. Jim was a social services worker and Leslie an electronics engineer. After their daughter,

Lauren, was born, she was placed in daycare in the caregiver's home while both parents continued to work. The situation was more stable than most daycare: Lauren only switched caregivers once in the two years during which she was cared for outside the home. But for Jim, that wasn't good enough.

Although Leslie found their arrangement more than satisfactory, especially considering the quality care they felt Lauren received, Jim felt a growing sense of dissatisfaction that they were not doing the right thing. Every time he dropped his daughter off, he felt a tightening in the pit of his stomach. He discussed it with his wife, but since Lauren was thriving and they were both successful at work, Leslie felt Jim was overreacting. Friends and co-workers tried to convince him that it was work-related stress that was causing his anxiety.

Jim sought help through his company's employee assistance plan and with a counselor's help, looked at the issue from multiple perspectives. Even though his own feelings were enough to convince him to stay home, he found another reason that he knew would be extremely compelling to Leslie. At his counselor's suggestion, Jim broke down the family's budget and income and discovered, to his shock, that after all Lauren's childcare costs and his work-related expenses, he was bringing home a mere $5,000 a year. Even though this was not an economic decision as far as Jim was concerned, he knew the financial facts would help convince Leslie.

Jim presented all this to Leslie, concluding that one of them needed to stay home full-time, and he was willing to be that person. Leslie agreed, and Jim became a full-time at-home dad. Now, son Gabriel has joined the family, and Jim looks after both kids and takes care of their home. He's never looked back.

Jim credits the open discussion style he and Leslie have developed for their ongoing "evolution of understanding" about their roles and relationship. Early in their marriage, they participated in the Roman Catholic Church's Marriage Encounter program, which helped them learn to communicate openly and honestly. Maybe the most valuable lesson for Jim was learning to ask who felt most passionately about a circumstance or situation.

Childcare was one of those issues for Jim. This is not to say that the children's welfare was not of primary importance to Leslie as well. It was. But Jim felt a passionate conviction that he and Leslie should do whatever was necessary so that one of them could be a full-time parent. And because he had such strong feelings about it, he did his economic and emotional homework, demonstrating to Leslie why it was right for their family and how it would work. That's the passion of involved fatherhood.

Reason #4—Mom Passionately Wants to Work

"It's a lot easier taking care of a fussy client than a fussy three-year-old."
    —Elizabeth, attorney, on pulling an all-nighter with her toddler

Here are three clues to help you figure out if you are a "warrior wife," a working mom who prefers the role of career woman to that of caretaker—whose primary focus is on providing rather than on homemaking.

1. You can find your way around a courtroom, factory, or office but are practically lost in your own kitchen or the kids' rooms.
2. You have to ask your husband how to operate the washing machine.
3. You prefer the business section to the food section in your newspaper.

Guess what? You're not alone.

In this group of SAHD/WM families, the at-home husbands run the household, care for the children, and, just as often, care for their working wives, too. Warrior wives are not like most working moms, who do manage to balance their dual work-family commitments fairly easily. These moms are passionately committed to their careers and generally devote enormous time and energy to them. And they often find they have more in common with their working-father counterparts than they do with other working moms, who may not share their ambition or drive. Frequently, the price of that dedication is a sense of guilt and sometimes even shame over what they themselves perceive as a diminished maternal instinct. What, they wonder, is wrong with them that they have trouble coping with a colicky baby, but can handle the stress of an intense workplace negotiation without batting an eye?

Warrior moms usually love to work and thrive on the stimulation, recognition, and rewards they receive from their jobs. Some freely admit they have little patience for full-time childrearing and are thrilled that their spouses are happy in that role. They panic at the thought of their husband going away for the weekend and leaving them to fend, not just for themselves—they could manage that—but for themselves *and* the kids. Around the clock, as in 24/7. No office, no lunch dates, no assistant. Just Mom and the kids.

Elizabeth, forty-three, is one of those women. She's an associate at a law firm, doing work that she loves and considers important. She is well compensated and well regarded in her field. When she and her husband, Nathan, got married, they knew they both wanted to have children. But at the time, it just seemed like an abstract concept, so they never really made any concrete decisions about who would be caring for those children. Six years later, they had their daughter, Sarah. They could have lived on Nathan's salary as a college professor, albeit in a scaled-back way, so finances were were not the deciding factor.

Nathan was as willing to stay home as Elizabeth was eager to keep working. She was relieved that he felt this way, because Elizabeth admits that she would have been torn about putting Sarah in daycare, but that she also would not have wanted to abandon a career she loved. She says that a closely supervised live-in nanny might have been an acceptable alternative. But it was never a serious option, since Nathan was opposed to daycare in any form and quite willingly set aside his career, at least for five or six years, so he could care for Sarah while Elizabeth continued at her firm.

For them, it has been a very livable solution. Sarah, now four, is thriving under Nathan's care, and Elizabeth is on the brink of making partner, something she's worked hard to achieve. They've split up their household and child-rearing tasks, and although Nathan handles by far the larger share, Elizabeth is also very much involved in their family's day-to-day life and very connected to her daughter.

Reason #5—Dad Can Work at Home

"I could probably make a lot more working for somebody else, but I wouldn't be there to pick Tucker up after school, to give him money for the ice cream truck . . ."
                    —Jay Massey, web developer, on why he works at home

When Jay's wife, Joann, discovered she was pregnant, there was no question about whether or not one of them would stay home with their child. A close-knit couple, both Jay and Joann had been raised by full-time moms and felt very strongly that one parent needed to be there for their kids. Nor was there any question about which of them would be that full-time parent. Joann had recently earned her doctorate in psychology, begun a new job, and amassed, as Jay described it, "a student loan the size of most people's first mortgages."

Jay, meanwhile, was in the planning stages of a new Internet marketing and design business. In the business's early development phase, he worked at a temp agency to bring in income. Since Jay had the flexibility and Joann had the stability, it just made good sense that he would be the stay-at-home parent. According to Jay, the decision was simple. They found out Joann was pregnant, and that very day Jay decided he'd stay home to raise their child. During the pregnancy, Jay continued to work temp jobs rather than commit himself to a full-time post, knowing that he would be leaving in a few months. But one company found his skills so valuable, they hired him full-time, on a short-term basis until his son was born.

Neither Jay nor Joann had any doubt that, despite their career ambitions, both would be involved parents. Joann stayed home for a brief maternity leave, then returned to work, eventually cutting down to a four-day work week so she could have more time at home with their son, Tucker. Jay simply modified his business plan, making his work home-based and using a less aggressive approach. He ended up nurturing a child and a business at precisely the same time and, although he has no second thoughts about his role as an at-home dad, Jay admits he might not have tackled both undertakings simultaneously if he had it to do all over again. What he and Joann lacked in sleep, however, they gained in satisfaction, knowing they were doing the right thing for Tucker.

Reason #6—Dad Is a Shift Worker

"I never really thought of myself as a stay-at-home dad, since I have a job; but I'm home more than most parents, working or not."
—Vince, firefighter, on working a two-days-on, four-days-off schedule

Thousands of shift workers, from firefighters to police officers to factory employees, spend several days in a row at their jobs, then the same amount of time, or more, at home, often caring for their kids. A typical schedule for firefighters, for example, is two days on, during which time they live at the station, then four days off, during which many of them stay home and care for their children. Many of these shift workers have working spouses who purposely design their schedules so that a full-time parent is home with the kids at all times. Both parents work what are essentially full-time jobs, albeit with slightly unusual schedules.

Vince and Lorena have just such an arrangement. Married for fourteen years, they have two daughters, ages thirteen and eleven. Vince is a firefighter and Lorena is a nurse. Both work full-time, but are able to arrange their shifts so that each of them can stay home and care for their girls on their off-time. They rarely use outside help. Vince considers it especially important that a parent be there for the girls at this stage of their lives because he believes that the teen and preteen years, when many parents begin to leave kids unsupervised for long periods of time, are precisely the time kids need guidance, discipline, and role models in the home. As he says, "quality time is a myth since you never know when a quality moment is going to pop up." Time itself is what's important, and that's what he and Lorena provide.

Their biggest concern is having enough "couple time" for themselves. It's especially hard for shift workers with opposite schedules to find time together, but Vince and Lorena recognize it as an issue. When they feel they haven't spent enough time together, Lorena usually drops a shift at the hospital, an easier scheduling maneuver for her than for Vince, and the two of them get a baby-sitter and go out for the night. Once the girls are in college, Vince and Lorena plan to make their schedules overlap so that they are both working and both off at the same times. In the meantime, they're there for their girls, and that's what's most important to them.

Your Reason for Becoming a SAHD/WM Family

Did you recognize yourself somewhere in there? Maybe you're the dad who passionately wants to be home with your kids. Or maybe you're the mom whose family benefits from your health benefits. Whatever your reasons, and sometimes there are several, it's never too early—or too late—to discuss your expectations and negotiate your roles. If you're considering becoming a SAHD/WM family, or even if you already are, it's time for some heavy-duty planning. That way, you'll have some idea where you're headed. And you can really enjoy the process. So let's move on to Chapter 3 and get busy drafting your "business plan" for a successful stay-at-home dad and working mom family!

Quick Review

This chapter introduces us to the primary reasons men choose to stay home and to some of the couples who've successfully launched their own SAHD/WM lifestyles.

Kids are the key.

Though there are lots of factors that contribute to the decision to try the SAHD/WM option, the primary reason for virtually every family exploring this lifestyle choice is because of the kids. These passionately involved couples believe that their children come first and that no one can parent as effectively as a parent.

There are six top reasons why Dad stays home with the kids.

1. Dad is out of work or makes significantly less than Mom.
2. Mom's job offers health benefits and/or stability and Dad's doesn't.
3. Dad passionately believes in being a stay-at-home parent.
4. Mom passionately wants to pursue her career.
5. Dad can work at home and still be a full-time parent.
6. Dad (and sometimes Mom, too) is a shift worker who cares for the kids in his off-hours.

The most important SAHD/WM reason of all.

Your reason, or reasons, are the most important of all. Read through the parenting profiles in Chapter 2 and see if any of these parents' experiences might apply to you as you rewrite the rules for your family.

Chapter 3

Your Business Plan for Becoming a Stay-at-Home Dad and Working Mom Family

Samuel didn't plan on being a stay-at-home dad. But after his wife, Jeannie, had to have an emergency cesarean section, and then more surgery for complications from the birth, Samuel decided to stay home to care for both of them. After all, he was at a transition point in his career and nothing was more precious to him than his wife and child. A year and a half later, with Jeannie long since recovered and their son an active toddler, Samuel realized that their temporary arrangement had somehow slid into a permanent lifestyle. Not that he regretted it, exactly; he just wondered if there might have been a better, more thoughtful way to set up their life.

S o you think you and your mate are ready to rewrite the traditional roles—to become a stay-at-home dad and working mom? Congratulations! But be forewarned: it's not for the overly conventional or less than adventurous. And since you're at the starting gate of a new way of life, there are few role models to follow. This chapter will help you create your own roadmap for arriving at the at-home dad/working mom lifestyle that is best suited to your particular family.

Couples who have succeeded say they have experienced stability and satisfaction unlike anything they'd known before they made the switch. Just making the commitment to determine your family's fate, instead of reacting to whatever life throws at you, can in itself be profoundly empowering. And shaping your lifestyle to suit your unique needs, talents, and goals can help reinforce your sense of yourselves as a couple, even as it helps you fulfill your individual desires. Best of all, your children will continue to reap the residual rewards long after you've both returned to the work force. Just be aware that you are venturing into uncharted territory, so honor the traveler's motto "Know before you go" and do some planning before you set off.

Although stay-at-home dads are a select group of approximately 2½ million men at the forefront of an evolutionary breakthrough in traditional gender roles, which will ultimately reshape the families and workplaces of our country, most of them (along with their wives) admit that they've taken on this new role with far less advance planning than they would use to buy a new car, plan a vacation, or remodel their kitchen.

Even couples who meticulously map out their retirement plans or conduct exhaustive research to find the perfect preschool fall into the "It just worked out that way" syndrome when it comes to determining their family's lifestyle structure. So, get ready to do some soul-searching and to open up the channels of communication between you and your spouse to discuss what is *really* best for your family. You may even have to strip away some of your prejudices and preconceptions about femininity and masculinity. But hey, if you and your partner can't *talk* about a lifestyle change, how are you going to live it?

The Family Start-up:
Preliminary Questions

You and your spouse wouldn't even *think* about starting up a business together without some semblance of a plan. It might not be a sophisticated or even highly detailed plan, but you would certainly have some sense of what each of your roles would be, how much money your start-up would require, and who would handle other family obligations during business hours. Becoming a stay-at-home dad and working mom family is actually a bit like starting a business; your ultimate "product" is a relationship that makes all parties—Mom, Dad, and the kids—happy.

You don't need an MBA to realize that all your family start-up plan actually requires is common sense, communication, and a little consideration for one another. Since we're designing *your* family structure to *your* specifications, you'll need to be honest about yourselves as individuals, as a couple, and as members of a family. If putting yourself under the microscope feels a little unnatural at first, chalk that up to your trailblazing status. Few couples, whether they're planning on reversing roles or not, subject their relationships to this sort of scrutiny. But give it a try; every marriage can benefit from some honest reflection and dialogue.

The first thing you need to do is ask yourselves the tough questions. A role-reversed lifestyle, even when it's running smoothly, can be tricky. If you're not prepared to take the knocks—or if you think your marriage might not be strong enough to withstand them—a nontraditional structure may not be for you. You'll need to discuss these life-altering changes in detail with your spouse and decide if you are suited for what can be threatening to our traditional concepts of both maleness and motherhood. It should be noted that although, ideally, you'd like to be able to count on the support of parents, in-laws, friends, and co-workers, a change in your life can also be threatening to other people's status quo. So don't assume everyone will be on your team.

Start by answering the following questions about yourself. Then answer them as you think your spouse would respond. Ask your partner to do the same; then swap and compare answers. You might be surprised at what you discover about yourself and each other.

The Family Start-up Preliminary Questionnaire

1. *Is your marriage sturdy enough to withstand switching traditional gender roles?* Really give some thought to this core issue. Are you a close, loving couple? Do you genuinely care about each other's success, happiness, and well-being? Do you feel you're in a stable, solid place in your life as a couple? If you're going through a difficult time in your marriage or are experiencing a transition such as a new job, a move, or an illness in the family, you need to consider whether you really want to take on the added challenge of swapping gender roles at this stage. It might be that you're better off maintaining your current lifestyle for the time being and revisiting role reversal once your situation stabilizes.

2. *Can you and your mate discuss problems openly and honestly?* If one or both of you are inclined to withdraw or overreact when problems arise, you may have to hone your communication skills before you take the role-reversal plunge. Remember that you'll be entering a sort of parallel universe: you'll likely encounter alien feelings and situations, which you and your spouse must be able to discuss on a regular, ongoing basis. If you're prepared to tackle issues as they arise, and to deal openly and fairly with each other's feelings, this new "experiment" can strengthen your relationship.

3. *Who do you honestly think is better suited to care for your children?* Ouch. This question can be very threatening, particularly to women, because it challenges our conventional views of motherhood. Many of us still cling to the traditional notion that moms are best at providing the quality care. It's not always easy to acknowledge that dads can be at least

as good as moms at being parents. But it's time to shake up some of those male/female stereotypes. We've finally accepted that women are capable workers and wage-earners; isn't it about time to let men have their due—and our respect—as caregivers? Consider all the basics here: loving and nurturing temperament, patience, sheer physical stamina, natural inclination to be a teacher, and, of course, the ability to disregard all forms of bodily fluid.

4. *Who has the more stable, gratifying, and/or lucrative job?* As we saw in Chapter 1, most couples choose the SAHD/WM family structure because they don't want their kids in daycare, but also because of financial considerations. Assuming that you're both working, you'll need to give some thought as to which of you is the more career-driven and ambitious. Ask yourselves who finds greater satisfaction and gratification in work. Or is it about the same for each of you? Are you both passionate about your careers, but still committed to having a full-time parent at home? All else being equal, if she has the bigger paycheck and/or the heftier benefits, that might make your decision.

   If you're a working dad/at-home-mom family, but open to switching places, think about what compromises you'll have to make concerning work and family. How does Dad feel about putting his career on hold? And how does Mom feel about returning to, or entering, the workplace? Better to think about all this now, rather than taking action and thinking about it later.

5. *Is Dad prepared to redefine his concept of masculinity?* No matter how loving and involved a parent might be, it's a whole new ballgame when Dad becomes *At-Home* Dad. When it suddenly dawns on him that he never goes to work but is on the job twenty-four hours a day. When laundry detergent and Play-Doh become much more important than power tools or power lunches. When stay-at-home moms eye him suspiciously, and former colleagues look on him with amusement. So don't underestimate what a serious

adjustment this role can be for men who have been socialized to succeed at work, but rarely at home.

Take Samuel and Jeannie, for example, the couple we
met in Chapter 2. They fell into the SAHD/WM life when
Jeannie suffered serious complications after their son's birth.
At first, Samuel reveled in his role as the primary caregiver,
looking after both his child and recuperating wife. But eventually, when Jeannie returned to work and became the family
breadwinner, their reversed lifestyle caught up with him, and
Samuel was surprised at how conflicted he felt. Finally, he
sought the counsel of a marriage and family therapist to help
him deal with the negative feelings which he feared were
affecting his marriage. On the one hand, he loved the time
he spent together with his son, Dylan. On the other, he felt
powerless and demeaned by relinquishing financial control
to his wife. Gradually, Samuel and Jeannie were able to find a
balance, which included part-time work for Samuel and a plan
for his full-time career reentry in another year. The real win-
ner, of course, was Dylan, who would continue to be cared
for at home by a parent until he was ready for preschool.

The Family Business Plan

So you've made it past the preliminary questions and you
and your spouse are speaking as honestly as you ever have. Maybe
you're even speaking to each other on a much deeper level
because you recognize a shared commitment to your children that
surpasses even your innate skepticism about this whole notion of
role-swapping. In fact, your family's well-being is so important to
you, you will even subject yourself to answering a bunch of prob-
ing questions if it might actually enhance the quality of your family life.

Michael and Susanna are just such a couple. They've recently
launched a direct-mail business, and as part of their business
launch have decided to swap parenting roles. Since Susanna is an

accomplished marketing executive, she will run the company while Michael serves as primary caregiver for their two young children, working ten hours a week from their home office. So, just as they've done with their company business plan, they're going to draw up a "business plan" for their family's role-reversal start-up.

Although some of the following steps may seem pretty obvious, it's surprising how few couples actually take the time to think about, discuss, or commit to paper their expectations and objectives. And even though few families experience the emotional upheaval that Samuel and Jeannie did when they reversed gender roles, the principle is the same for everyone. Instead of sliding into a role-reversed lifestyle and risking problems down the road, *take the time to plan for success.*

Your Family Mission Statement

The first step is to identify just what it is you hope to accomplish by reversing traditional roles. Call it a mission statement, a vision, an objective, a goal—call it whatever you like, but make sure you incorporate answers to the following questions. There are no right and wrong answers; just be honest and clear.

- What do my spouse and I hope to gain by switching gender roles and establishing Mom as the primary breadwinner and Dad as the at-home caretaker?
- What are our priorities for our family?
- What are our priorities as a couple?
- What are our priorities as individuals?

If your objective is really to save money because you feel that your daycare is costing you a fortune and shortchanging your children, state that. If your goal is to have a parent at home full-time, and Dad wants it to be him because he never got to know his own dad growing up, make sure you acknowledge that. If your vision includes letting Mom soar in her career, while Dad keeps home and family running like a well-oiled machine, out with it. Whatever motivated you to buy this book in the first place is your first clue. Don't overlook the obvious, but don't ignore the subtext either.

Whether you undertake this exercise individually or in tandem, you and your spouse should agree on your family's mission statement. Even if one of you is the driving force in your lifestyle overhaul and the other has agreed to go along for the ride, don't think you can successfully create this plan in a vacuum. You need consensus; in business they call it buy-in, and in this context it means that both you and your spouse have to buy the philosophy and the practice of role-reversal in order for the family to achieve its goal. Once you've reached an agreement about your objective, write it down. The statement doesn't have to be long or involved. In fact, it shouldn't be. Just a few declarative statements or a short paragraph about what it is you hope to achieve in your as-yet-theoretical SAHD/WM lifestyle.

Michael and Susanna's family mission statement reads as follows:

Family will always be our first priority. We will honor that commitment by having a full-time parent care for our children, at least until they reach elementary school age. For now, subject to change in the future, Michael will be the primary caregiver and Susanna will be the primary wage-earner. As long as it is financially feasible, our business will be located in our community so that Susanna will not have to commute and can leave work as necessary to attend family or school functions. Michael will continue to work part-time from home in order to help build the business and to keep his skills up-to-date so he will be ready to work full-time in the future.

Clearly, the priority for Michael and Susanna is their family, and they have carefully constructed a lifestyle that will support their children's needs. Childcare experts would applaud. And Michael and Susanna have managed to meet their children's needs without sacrificing their own. Through careful planning and painstaking prioritization, they've enabled Michael to care for their children full-time as Susanna builds their business. They've also planned

for Michael's eventual career reentry and allowed for him to maintain his skills by working part-time.

Not that it's all going to be a piece of cake. Success will call for
hard work, dedication, and some artful juggling on Michael and
Susanna's part. But imagine the millions of two-career couples
who would welcome such a challenge if only they recognized role
reversal as a viable option.

One such couple are Gary and Elise, who had two careers and
three kids under age ten when Gary was laid off because his plant
closed. He intended to find a new job as quickly as possible, but
when he discovered how much he enjoyed being home with the
children and how dramatically the quality of the kids' lives—as
well as his and Elise's—improved under the guidance of a full-time
parent, he began to apply the same budgeting constraints on the
family that he'd used on the job. With judicious planning and by
eliminating a few extras, they became a one-career family, and
Gary stayed home for the next seven years. Although they made
their role reversal work, Gary admits that he and Elise would have
saved themselves a lot of grief early on if they had spent more time
defining their roles and less time arguing about them. After several
such frustrating and fruitless fights, Gary finally decided to adopt
another simple management technique: the job description.

Your Job Descriptions

Now that you've stated your mission, it's time to write a comprehensive job description for each of you, detailing precisely what
your roles are with regard to career, household duties, and parenting. There are several ways you can attack this exercise. Each of you
can write a description of your individual role, then compare to
make sure you are in agreement and that nothing has fallen
between the cracks of the two descriptions. Or you can each draft
your own descriptions of the working mom and at-home dad roles,
then discuss and synthesize them. This method gives you the
advantage of mapping out exactly what you can see as your own
and each other's roles without being influenced by each other until

you've detailed everything as thoroughly as you can on your own. Or, of course, you can draft the working mom and at-home-dad descriptions together, discussing your expectations as you go.

The job descriptions can be as simple as a list of job duties or as detailed as a formal contract. Obviously, the more complete they are, the better the foundation on which to build your role-reversal start-up plan. But be careful not to assume anything. If in doubt, spell it out. And be sure to consider not only schedules but preferences when assigning tasks. For example, if Mom loathes grocery shopping but loves to cook, make sure you factor that in. And if Dad is happy to do the gardening but wants a cleaning person to come in a couple of times a month, indicate that in your plan. Remember, this is an exercise in realistic life planning, not torture. Job titles to consider within your descriptions, but not limit yourself to, might include the following.

Caregiver. If Dad is the primary caregiver, what are his hours? Do they end when Mom comes home from work? And approximately what time would that be? What are the specific kid-care responsibilities of each parent—for instance, does Dad take care of the kids during the day, but Mom is in charge of bath and bed routines? Or does Dad take weekdays, while Mom is in charge on Saturdays and Sundays? You'll need to discuss parenting styles, if you haven't already, and agree upon a consistent approach. It's important to acknowledge that men and women often have different ways of reaching the same result (see Chapter 6). Just remember it's always the welfare of your children that should shape your approach.

Wage Earner. If Mom is the wage earner, what are her anticipated hours? Does Dad also work outside the home (or at home in a wage-earning capacity), and if so, for how many hours a week? How will business travel affect child care, if at all? Is there a plan for Dad to return to the workforce in the future? Will Mom become the primary caregiver at some point, and, if so, when might that happen? You may not have all the answers right now, but it's never too early to start asking the questions, such as

"When will Dad make his reentry into the work world?" If he's concerned, as he'd have every right to be, about stepping off the career path, this could be just the reassurance that he needs.

Educator. If you believe, as most parents do, that education is a critical component of a child's upbringing, then you and your spouse need to determine how each of you can play an active role in your child's schooling. Who is in charge of supervising homework? Who will serve as the primary school contact, volunteering in the classroom or driving the carpool? And if Dad, as primary caregiver, assumes these roles, how will Mom remain an active participant in the educational process?

Since volunteering in the classroom is usually the domain of at-home moms, at-home dads need to consider their strengths and comfort levels in school volunteering situations. You might even consider following in the footsteps of Hogan, the innovative stay-at-home dad from Irvine, California, whom we met in Chapter 2. Hogan founded Dads in Action to identify specific jobs, from developing a reading program to building bookshelves, that could encourage greater dad involvement in his child's school. He not only created a more meaningful and comfortable role for himself in his child's education, but also paved the way for other dads in his community to become more involved.

Social Director. You'll need to decide which one of you is going to lead the charge with regard to the family's social calendar. Who keeps track of play dates, plans birthday parties, and buys gifts? Which one of you will be the primary contact with your extended family, organizing plans and schedules for visits, outings, and holidays? You'll also want to consider your involvement—both participation and scheduling—in organizations and community activities, which can be an invaluable anchor to your neighborhood as well as a great growth opportunity for your kids.

And don't overlook vacation planning. Heaven forbid! For work-weary moms, dads on the verge of burnout, and kids eager for new experiences, vacations are an important part of family life.

Vacation planning can be a rewarding family activity, depending on the ages of your children, or one or both parents can be in charge. Just make sure you include vacation planning somewhere in your description because, trust me, you're going to need it.

Housekeeper. Is this job split between Mom and Dad? If so, how are tasks divided? If it's Dad's sole responsibility, does he do it all by himself, or is there outside help? Is Mom responsible for specific housekeeping jobs? And are there certain jobs that each spouse enjoys or insists on doing as a matter of survival? Even the most accomplished at-home dads often admit to lacking the gene for laundering fine washables. After they've turned a few loads of laundry that tell-tale pink, they're usually all too happy to relinquish that particular task to Mom or the professionals.

So if Mom wants to lay claim to laundry or shopping for the kids' back-to-school clothes, put it in your job description. Conversely, Dad may prefer to be the exclusive user of the power tools. While role reversal does imply a blurring of gender stereotypes, it doesn't negate the fact that some jobs are often preferred by women, others by men. However, if he'd rather wash dishes than wash the car and she'd rather shovel snow than shop, by all means recognize that in your plan.

And don't forget to assign household chores to the kids once they're old enough. In fact, the younger the child, the more enthusiastic he or she usually is about pitching in. (See Chapter 10 for tips on getting the kids involved in household chores.)

Cook. Who does the cooking? Will the cook be "on duty" every day, or have a couple of days off per week? Is cooking to be a shared responsibility, with Dad doing breakfast and lunch, and Mom doing dinner? Maybe Dad is in charge of cooking during the week, but Mom takes over on weekends. Or Dad cooks, but Mom bakes. Whatever works for you is the right recipe for your family.

Grocery Shopper. Who is responsible for shopping? Does one parent "own" this activity or is it a shared responsibility? Is there a grocery-list system in effect that places some of the responsibility on the nonshopping spouse as well as the kids? If your kids are old enough to participate, explain your list system and grocery budget to them. It's never too early to share in the decision-making.

Accountant. Conscientiousness is the key here, so whoever is the bigger stickler for paying the bills on time should get this job. It's usually advisable for one parent to take primary responsibility for paying bills and tracking finances so neither one assumes the *other* is handling it. But both of you should actively participate in big-picture financial planning for retirement, investing, and college savings.

Errand Runner. While this may seem to fall in the Dad domain, it's an easy spot for Mom to pick up some slack. She can do one less business lunch every week or so, or leave the office a half-hour early on occasion to relieve Dad of some of his schlepping duties. And for moms who travel or work very long hours, errands that include the kids can add some extra face time to your schedule. Save the haircuts, shoe shopping, and trips to the mall for weekends with the kids. Just expect it to take twice as long and be half as productive as if you were going it alone. Better yet, take the kids to the zoo and let Dad do a couple of errands that he actually enjoys, then take the rest of the day off for himself. That way everyone wins.

Now that you've covered the basics of your job description, take a few minutes to personalize the list for your family. Consider religious education, music lessons, after-school clubs, sports activities, time with relatives, special medical needs, and anything else that makes this a custom blueprint for your family. Also include any qualifiers like time off for Dad—say, one night a week or a weekend every three to six months—and any other stipulations not covered by your specific job duties.

Then, just as you would do on the job, sit down with your spouse and periodically review your lifestyle plan, formally, just as in a performance appraisal at work. Take out your mission statement and your job descriptions and look over them. Did your outcomes match your expectations? If not, why not? What can you change to make your roles more equitable and satisfying? Is there a job you or your spouse has come to dread that the other can willingly take on? Or should some responsibility—like heavy-duty cleaning or fixing the car—be farmed out to hired help? For most couples, a solid discussion every three months will probably suffice, but it's entirely up to you. If you and your mate want to review your joint performance over a glass of Chardonnay every other Saturday night, that's the spirit!

That's a Plan!

Congratulations. You've now written a mission statement articulating your lifestyle objectives and identifying how role reversal can revolutionize your family life. You've also drafted detailed job descriptions for each spouse, defining your work and parenting obligations. You've listed not only who does what, but when and how they do it. You've even answered all those nagging questions about who takes out the trash and who makes brownies for the first-grade bake sale. And you've challenged about a zillion gender stereotypes in the process.

When Kim and Levi first sat down to draft their mission statement, they discovered they had completely different takes on why they were planning their role reversal. Kim thought it was because Levi wanted a chance to stay home with their twins, but also because he had lost his enthusiasm for teaching and wasn't sure what to do next. Levi thought it was because Kim was anxious to pursue her career in a brokerage firm and not so excited about caring for twin toddlers.

After they talked through their misconceptions, they realized that both were partially right and that each of them was much more flexible about their future plans than the other had thought. Kim was eager to structure "mom time" into her life and to scale back her work schedule at some future point. And Levi was committed to returning to the workforce sooner than Kim had thought. Their mission statement synthesized both points of view, as follows:

> *Our shared work-family goal is for Levi to be home full-time with Marc and Mallory for the next five years, until they are ready for first grade. Until then, Kim will be the primary provider, working full-time (but avoiding travel if at all possible). At that time, Kim will reduce her schedule to a 30-hour week (moving to a more "family friendly" company if necessary). Levi will return to teaching, probably on a part-time basis. At that point, we may consider outside help (daycare or nanny) as a part-time option.*

Having clarified their feelings about their individual commitments to child-rearing and their careers, they were able to much more accurately reflect their family mission.

Ben and Madeleine found the mission-statement portion of the business plan to be fairly straightforward. When Ben's restaurant went out of business just as Madeleine landed her dream job as a news director at a local television station, the result was pretty clear. He was staying home with their son, Andy, and she was going to work. What was tricky was splitting up their job descriptions. The cooking part was easy; that had always been Ben's domain. But when it came to other household responsibilities, things broke down and the couple had a hard time splitting up tasks. Finally, they decided to have some fun with the process, and their plan began to flow. Madeleine and Ben created entirely new work categories and split their list up like this:

Ben	*Madeleine*
Childcare guy	School volunteer (as able)
Chef	Kids' wardrobe mistress

Ben	Madeleine
Manager of cleaning crew (1x/wk)	Weekend soccer mom & chauffeur
Grocery shopper	In-law handler
Keeper of master schedule	Bill payer

Not to worry: whatever works is what's right for you. Most of those 2½ million SAHD/WM couples probably experienced something very similar to what you're going through. In fact, it would be a little weird if you had no concerns at all, wouldn't it? So here are a few words of encouragement from the experts: those at-home dads already in the trenches, as well as their hardworking wives. Because no one is more sympathetic to what you're contemplating.

Eight Commandments from the SAHD/WMS (they were too busy for ten)

Be sure that your stay-at-home dad decision comes from the heart, and it's not just a logical or financial move. It may be prompted by those rational considerations, but it must be accompanied by a deep sense that this is the right thing to do. Even if it is forced upon you by a layoff or other external circumstance, it can only work as long as you stay in touch with the feeling that you are doing something important, whether others recognize it or not.

Expect dads to do things differently from moms. Women ask for directions. Men use tools. Face it, men and women *are* different, in their parenting styles as well as in other ways, and their differences should be recognized and embraced. By trusting their own instincts, at-home dads have come up with some ingenious methods of discipline and child care that their feminine counterparts might never have dreamed of. There's the at-home dad who changes his infant daughter in the carpeted trunk of the car. Or the dad who uses cereal for tinkle target practice for his son's potty training. Then there's the dad who has theme days—like Backwards Day, when he and his preschoolers wear all their clothes backwards and eat dinner in the morning and breakfast at night— to keep the kids occupied and entertained.

Make time for yourself. Living well is the best revenge, and for at-home dads, "living well" means taking time out for activities that you enjoy. *What* you do doesn't really matter that much; it's the doing of it that counts. Even if it feels forced at first, be sure to keep up with hobbies, workouts, and friendships. Leave the kids with Grandma or at a neighbor's every now and then, and take the time to ride your bike, play golf, or just have lunch with a couple of old friends. Relax; no one's expecting you to be a martyr. Don't expect it of yourself.

Take pride in your job. So what if you're the only guy who drives the school carpool? Or the only dad who participates in your daughter's Brownie troop? If you think it's weird, others probably will, too. But if you act as if being a full-time, involved, and loving father is the greatest gift on earth, then everyone else will see it that way, too.

Remember that stay-at-home moms are your comrades in arms. Never forget that at-home moms are your colleagues. Besides other at-home dads, who might just be scarce in your neighborhood, they're the only ones who really understand what you're going through, how you spend your days and what gets Enfamil stains out of white T-shirts. You're shy, you say? Well, get over it. Introduce yourself to that nice mom you see in the park every afternoon. You can use your kids as conversation starters. They won't mind.

Be aware that you're part of an evolutionary process. Gender roles, and our preconceptions about them, really are starting to change. If you don't believe it, just look around your neighborhood. More dads than ever before are dropping their kids off at school. Better yet, dads are volunteering at school and attending school functions in record numbers. And activities that used to have truly sexist names like "Mom & Tots" or "Music with Mommy" are finally acknowledging that Dad might take an interest in his kids' activities. So they're changing their names to "Parents & Tots." Or "Mom & Dad & Music." And, finally, the most dad-friendly development of all: more changing tables in men's rooms than ever before. Is that progress or what?

Never forget that dads still drive. Take heart, guys, this is not just anecdotal. There is hard scientific evidence to support the fact that even in families with full-time, at-home dads and working moms, dads still drive the family car 80 percent of the time. And guess what? It's virtually the same as in households where Dad is the breadwinner and Mom stays home. With all the changes you go through to trade places, it's nice to know that some things, even the little things, never change.

Take heed of what the veteran SAHDs say: they wouldn't change their lifestyle for the world. In a recent survey of at-home dads, an overwhelming majority said that if they had it to do all over again, they wouldn't change a thing. Descriptions of their experiences as at-home dads include "Best experience of my life," "I learned to appreciate every day," and "Other dads don't know what they're missing." So what are you waiting for?

Quick Review

Let's recap what we've learned in this chapter about establishing a family start-up plan for at-home dads and working moms.

Ask yourselves the preliminary questions.

You and your spouse need to ask yourselves some tough questions and discuss them honestly before seriously considering a gender swap. Those questions include:

- Is your marriage tough enough to handle switching roles?
- Can you and your spouse discuss problems openly and honestly?
- Who do you think is better suited to care for your children?
- Whose career is more stable, lucrative, and/or fulfilling?
- Can Dad handle the blows to the male ego that role reversal can cause?

Create a family mission statement.

Identify your vision for your family, articulating your goals and objectives, in a concise sentence or two. You and your spouse should agree upon priorities for your family, even if you disagree about approach, before attempting to switch roles.

Draft detailed job descriptions for yourselves.

Just as most CEOs and secretaries have job descriptions detailing their duties, you and your spouse need to draft a comprehensive list of parenting and work obligations so that you can decide exactly who will do what. Consider childcare, housekeeping, cooking—all the basics—plus whatever is unique to your family. If in doubt, spell it out.

Establish periodic review times.

Agree upon how often you want to review your mission statement and job descriptions so you can make course corrections as you go. Setting up review times in advance, just as you would on the job, will force you to discuss your progress and any pitfalls you've encountered along the way.

You are not alone. There's plenty of encouragement and advice from the at-home-dad frontier. At-home dads have created newsletters, websites, and conventions to make things easier for the next guys in line. (See Appendix for Resource Guide.) Because they've already learned that what they're doing is not only worthwhile, it's the most important job they'll ever have.

Chapter 4

How to Make It on One Income, and Other Minor Miracles

Now that you are mentally prepared to start thinking about the stay-at-home dad/working mom lifestyle in business terms, it's time to consider your finances. So let's look at your budget and see how you might become a one-income family. And if you're already living on one wage, maybe you'll learn some painless new ways to stretch that family dollar even further.

Jennifer and Lawrence and their three boys, aged twelve, seven, and four, live in a pleasant but modest middle-class neighborhood in the suburbs just outside a major city. Jennifer is a full-time supervisor for a packaging company; Lawrence is a full-time stay-at-home dad. The family's annual household income is approximately $48,000. The older kids go to public school; the youngest goes to preschool. Except for an occasional Nintendo game their parents won't buy them because of its hefty pricetag, the kids have pretty much everything they want. And so do Jennifer and Lawrence: a nice house, money in the bank, a family vacation every summer and, most of all, a full-time parent at home with the kids.

Kathy and Mario, and their two daughters and son, also live in a middle-class neighborhood on the outskirts of a major city. Their annual household income is approximately $82,000. They also have two kids in public school and one in preschool, a nice house and a family vacation every summer. Kathy and Mario care about what's best for their children as much as Jennifer and Lawrence do, but they've bought into the myth that two incomes buy a better lifestyle. They say they'd love for one of them to give up their job and stay home full-time with the kids, but they just can't see how they can afford to lose the income.

Actually, the question is how Kathy and Mario can afford *not* to give up one of their paychecks, when the net income of single-career couples like Jennifer and Lawrence is actually at least as much as Mario and Kathy's incomes combined. Setting aside the incalculable value of having their kids cared for by an at-home parent, how is it that single-income Jennifer and Lawrence come out *financially* ahead of dual-income Kathy and Mario? Is this some kind of mathematical trick question?

It may surprise you, but most money experts will tell you that two-income families do not necessarily have a financial advantage over one-income families. Naturally, lifestyles and earnings vary widely from family to family, and many parents don't have the luxury of even entertaining the thought of giving up their jobs. But, just like Mario and Kathy, many two-career couples believe that second income is providing a better life for their families, but that might not necessarily be the case. In fact, as they're running themselves ragged, they may actually be spending more money on that second job than they're bringing home.

Yep, you heard it right. That second job may actually be *costing* them money. And if being home to take care of your kids isn't enough of a reason to convince you that your family can live on one income, maybe doing the math—and seeing it in black and white—will do the trick. Remember Jim and Leslie from Chapter 2? When Jim did their math, they were both shocked to discover that he was really bringing home a mere $5,000 after work-related and childcare expenses. And Jim and Leslie are far from alone in their financial situation. When both parents work, the childcare-related expenses and workplace costs add up very quickly. Compound that with all the "conveniences" that suddenly become necessities when both of you are busy all day long, and that second income starts trickling right down the drain.

Among those conveniences are cleaning services and take-out dinners. And while take-out dinners like Chinese food or broiled chicken with family-sized sides may provide more nutrition than fast food, they also cost a lot more. Many two-income couples also consider a regular cleaning or maid service a necessity. Time-challenged to begin with, these busy parents hardly want to spend their weekends cleaning the bathroom. Other conveniences include prepackaged goods or services, like all-in-one birthday parties that come with the works—entertainment, cake, goody bags—and a pricetag to match. Of course, for at-home parents, planning a party—or anything else that requires more time and imagination than it does money—can be as much fun for the kids as it is cost-effective for the budget.

Then, of course, there's the whole range of unavoidable career-related expenses like an appropriate work wardrobe, commuting costs, and restaurant lunches. Add to that the cost of childcare, and you can see how a job's pricetag begins to skyrocket.

The High Cost of Two Incomes

Kathy, a public health officer for the county, and Mario, a tile installer, mapped out two distinct scenarios for their family's finances, as well as a realistic monthly budget, including their childcare-related expenses. In one scenario both of them continued at their jobs and they remained a two-income family. The other assumed a full-time nonworking parent at home, either Mario or Kathy, depending on whoever was bringing in less in terms of salary and benefits. And, finally, they drafted a basic monthly budget so they would have a clear picture of their financial goals.

Scenario One: Mario and Kathy's Two-Income Plan

Gross income:	Mario	$35,000
	Kathy	47,000
Total gross income:		$82,000
Minus 10 percent for 401K contributions:	Mario	$3,500
	Kathy	4,700
Adjusted gross income:		$73,800
Minus estimated federal, state,		
and social security taxes of 30 percent:		$22,140
Family's total take-home pay		$51,660
Minus additional costs of dual incomes:		
Daycare		$10,200
Commuting		1,560
Lunches/coffee		2,600
Take-out/restaurants		2,400
Housekeeper/cleaning svc		2,000
Drycleaning		800
Net income:		$32,100

Scenario Two: Mario and Kathy's One-Income Plan

In this scenario, Mario will stay home as full-time parent, since Kathy's income is not only more stable but higher than this. This budget also allows for some part-time outside help, but no child-care expenses.

Gross income:	Kathy	$47,000
Total gross income:		$47,000
Minus 10 percent for 401K contributions:	Kathy	$4,700
Adjusted gross income:		$42,300

Minus estimated federal, state, and	
social security taxes of 30 percent:	$12,690
Family's total take-home pay	$29,610

Minus work-related/household expenses:	
Part-time cleaning	$1,200
Commuting	$780
Lunches/coffee	$1,300
Drycleaning	$600
Net income:	$25,730

Look closely at both scenarios. Are you surprised at the results? You may be, but most financial planners aren't, because they know that the cost of all those conveniences, which seem so necessary when both of you are working, can add up dramatically. But deduct the daycare, along with all those things like the premium-priced take-out dinners you're addicted to because neither of you has time to cook, or the cleaning service you just have to have because you don't want to spend your precious leisure hours scrubbing toilets, and you've saved almost an entire salary. And, unlike Mario who doesn't need fancy work clothes and doesn't have an expensive commute, think what you might save in wardrobe costs, dry cleaning, business lunches, and transportation costs.

Your Three-Step Budget Plan

So, now you've seen how one couple calculated the two-income and single-income scenarios. Mario and Kathy needed the cold, hard facts to supplement what, ultimately, was an emotional choice about childcare. But once they were armed with the figures and saw how little they would actually gain financially by continuing to pursue two incomes, their decision that Mario would stay home and become a full-time dad became much easier.

One additional thing you should be aware of: if Dad gives up his job and stays home, even for a limited period of time, he will forgo the wage increases and additional 401K savings that might have come with staying on the job. Like any working woman who gives up her job to stay home with kids, he'll also have to manage a career reentry later, including the inevitable explanation of where he's been all this time. Understanding—beforehand—that his skills and savings may not keep pace with his peers' while he's home with the little ones is just a reality of stay-at-home-dad life. Just don't lose sight of the intangible, nonmonetary rewards, like the incredible bond you build with your kids.

Now, let's look at your finances and see if we can give you some budgetary building blocks to help you with your family's financial structuring. If you're just now contemplating a role-reversed family, you'll need to make the best-informed decision that you can. If you're already living the at-home dad/working mom lifestyle, you'll still benefit from some budgetary formulas that can help make your role-reversal journey a little easier. So, just as Mario and Kathy did, let's start by mapping out your two-income and one-income scenarios.

Step One: Calculate Your Two-Income Scenario

Gross income:	His	$
	Hers	$
Total gross income:		$
Minus 10 percent for 401K contributions:	His	$
	Hers	$
Adjusted gross income:		$
Minus taxes:		
Federal		$
State		$
FICA		$
Family's Total Take-Home Pay		$

Minus additional costs of dual incomes:

Daycare	$
Commuting	$
Lunches/coffee	$
Take-out/restaurants	$
Housekeeper/cleaning svc	$
Other	$
Your Two-Career Net Income	$

If you're currently a two-career couple, the table above should reflect a pretty accurate picture of your current income. Did you add in all those extras that you've come to rely on as part of your two-job lifestyle? There may be others not even on that list, so be sure to put them down so you can get a realistic comparison of life with two incomes versus life with one.

Step Two: Calculate Your Single-Income Scenario

Scenario two assumes that you and your family will be living on the working mom's income. Dad may supplement this through part-time or work-at-home income, but we'll get to that a little later. For now, let's look at living solely on one income. In this scenario, you can take out all those additional expenses like childcare, high-priced take-out dinners, plus his commuting and other work-related costs, and all the other "convenience costs" associated with the two-wage lifestyle. Remember to leave in some budget dollars, however, if you still plan to use a cleaning service or a part-time sitter. Keep in mind that Dad's sanity is not a luxury item.

Gross income:	Her income	$
Total gross income:		$
Minus 10 percent for 401K contributions:	Hers	$
Adjusted Gross Income:		$

Minus taxes:	Federal	$
	State	$
	FICA	$
Family's Total Take-Home Pay		$
Minus household expenses:	Part-time cleaning	$
	Other	$
Your Single-Career Net Income:		$

Now compare the two. Even using conservative estimates for the additional costs of childcare and the expenses necessitated by both of you working outside the home, are these two scenarios close in terms of net income? It all goes to prove that, just as the financial experts say, for most couples with "average" incomes it may make sense, and cents, for him to stay home full-time.

Assuming that you're ready for the final step, let's move on to budgeting and see how much money you actually need to sustain your family's lifestyle.

Step Three: Budgeting for What You Really Need

Now that you have a clear picture of your income, let's make sure you plan adequately for your budget needs. Following is a blueprint you can follow. Note that it assumes that health insurance and medical costs are covered by the working mom's job. If not, include them. In fact, be sure to customize the entire budget to fit your family.

Your Family's Monthly Budget

Mortgage/Rent $
Car Payment $
    (*maintenance, gas, etc.*)
Utilities $
    (*electricity, phone, cell phone, Internet
    access, heat, water, cable, etc.*)

Insurance	$
(*auto, homeowners/renters*)	$
Food	$
Taxes	$
School	$
(*tuition, books, music lessons, etc.*)	
Entertainment	$
(*dinners out, movie tickets, baby-sitters*)	
Consumer Debt	
Savings	$
(*retirement, college funds*)	
Miscellaneous	$
Your Family's Monthly Budget	$

And there you have it in black and white: your family's entire financial picture, from income to budget. You've made it this far, so you're probably considering a one-wage lifestyle as a real possibility and the best means of providing—both emotionally and financially—for your future. What does it take to get ready? Or, if you're already living on one wage, how can you stretch those dollars even farther?

Welcome to Downsizing

No, we're not talking about corporate fat-trimming. We're talking about trimming the fat in your family's budget. And no matter how frugally you think you're living already, there are always a few places you can trim more easily than you'd assume. First and foremost, get into the right state of mind about your family's downsizing efforts. Most important, don't think of economizing as a kind of slow death from lack of luxuries and pampering. If you're stuck in "we're depriving ourselves" mode, you'll sabotage yourselves before you've even started. Instead, think of downsizing as healthy change that will promote what is most beneficial for your family, especially those kids you love more than anything in the world.

They'll be gaining a full-time, at-home parent who will be there when they wake up from a nap, come home from school, or need a ride to soccer practice. And even if Mom's working late, they'll always have Dad to tuck them in at night.

So look on your downsizing efforts as:

- An investment in your children's well-being
- A fun family project
- A time-limited experience (i.e., not a life sentence)
- A compromise, not a sacrifice

If your kids are old enough, get them involved in the spirit of saving. If they understand that you're concerned about saving because you want to make sure that a parent will always be there for them, they will get it. They'll also learn thrifty habits that can last them a lifetime and benefit their own children. They'll find out—the fun way—that a weekend at the lake can be just as memorable as a trip to Disney World. The beauty of such trade-offs is that kids rarely know the difference. Sure, Disney World would be fun, but they'll get there one of these days. In the meantime, they'll have a less flashy but equally exhilarating time at the lake, and a priceless bonus to boot: Dad at home taking care of them every single day. How can Mickey compare with that?

The first step in downsizing and preparing to live on one income is to take a good, clear look both at the budget you just prepared and at your income table. How do the two jibe? How much fat do you think you need to cut? Set some target goals and then decide with your mate where to cut back. We've already seen how conveniences like take-out dinners and cleaning services can hit your budget where it hurts. Now let's look at some other downsizing tips to see what might work for you.

Downsizing Budget Boosters

- Set up a babysitting co-op in the neighborhood. Save sitter costs *and* get an occasional night out.

- Join "frequent user" clubs, modeled after airline frequent-flyer programs for everything from videos to pantyhose.
- Look for bargains like early-bird dinners or bargain movie matinees.
- Become a market coupon clipper. The kids love this one, and not only do they learn about saving, they'll frequently try a new food *just* because they have a coupon.
- Buy in bulk. Always.
- Check books out of the library instead of buying them. Another great kid activity!
- Look in your local paper for listings of free weekend activities, like street fairs and cultural events.
- Forget the health club (unless it's an integral part of Dad's sanity plan) and take up running or biking.
- Shop in consignment stores for used baby/kid clothes, furniture, and toys. Or trade in *yours* for *theirs*.
- Check out books listed in the Resource Guide for their money-saving tips.
- Invest in a two- or three-year-old "new" car instead of a brand-new one.
- Search out the best public schools, rather than enrolling your kids in costly private ones.

Ted and Tamara had decided early on in their relationship that they would raise their kids themselves. Having two sets of young-at-heart grandparents right in the neighborhood also helped with their decision that Tamara would give up her job as an airline reservationist and stay home when the time came. But when the time did come and they were expecting their first child, Tamara had just been promoted to a management position and Ted was about to embark on a new career as a mortgage broker, working out of the house.

They did some serious thinking and came up with the following plan. Tamara would take a three-month maternity leave, and Ted would put off his new career venture for at least a year to care for their son. The eager grandparents would lend a hand, and Ted would use any downtime to start educating himself about the marketplace in preparation for his business launch.

The next step was to figure out where they might downsize. Already thrifty by nature, Ted and Tamara first whittled down their credit card debt until it was virtually nonexistent. For them, credit cards were something you kept on hand for emergencies, then paid off entirely each month. They refused to get caught in that high-interest minimum-payment cycle. Next, they cut back on costly luxuries like restaurant dinners and fancy take-out foods. Ted and Tamara shared cooking duties and, as a side benefit, began to eat more healthily too. Taking it a step further, Ted began to hit the shopping clubs and buy in bulk, often splitting purchases with the relatives when the bulk items were just too *bulky* for one family.

You get the picture. Look around your house, your garage, your kitchen. What can you live without? Chances are, you can spot lots of things you could give up, at least for a few years until both of you are working again. And isn't it worth it?

Emotional Finance

Of course, your family financial scenario isn't all dollars and cents. Picture this: A nice romantic restaurant. Soft lighting, maybe a little music in the background. Brad and Jillian, married nine years, have just finished a delicious Italian meal, polished off a bottle of wine, and moved on to their after-dinner coffee. It's just about time to go home. Brad's mom has been watching their toddler for the evening and they don't want to overstay their welcome with their favorite baby-sitter. Jill calls for the check, plops down her American Express card, and pays the bill.

A perfectly ordinary scenario for plenty of couples, including Jillian and Brad. But for others, especially for some money-sensitive stay-at-home dads, it's an awkward and unpleasant moment and one they've learned to associate with embarrassment—or worse, outright shame. Numerous stay-at-home dads report that one of the hardest adjustments to becoming an at-home father is dealing with their own conflicted emotions about money. More specifically, the loss of power and sense of emasculation that may accompany the decision to hand over the financial reins to the wife.

But do handing over the financial reins and loss of power necessarily go hand in hand? And is it true that just because Dad has decided to stay home and nurture, he is abdicating his economic decision-making power? Well, yes and no. It all depends on how well couples handle their "emotional finances." That is, how they feel about money, how well they articulate those feelings, and how successfully they negotiate the conflicts that will inevitably arise.

Put yourself in that restaurant for a moment. If you and your spouse were characters in that scenario, which of you would have paid the check? Would either of you have had a problem with that? Do you even know if your spouse is sensitive to this issue? Have you discussed who picks up the check and pays the bills, and have you talked about other power-related matters associated with who wields the wallet? In other words, how tuned in are you when it comes to emotional finance?

You've already tackled the nuts and bolts of budgets, but now let's look a little more deeply at our feelings about earning power, personal power, and self-worth. Working out a budget usually just comes down to common sense and math, and, with the right kind of communication and planning, it's generally pretty manageable for most couples. Where stay-at-home dads and working moms tend to trip up, as Brad and Jillian might have were they not so attuned to each other's financial feelings, is the emotional part.

For many of us, money means much more than just spending currency. It's all tied up with our sense of belonging, our feelings about what we deserve, our guilt over our abundance or lack of it. Why do you think so many couples fight about money? Because the topic is so loaded, clouded by our upbringing as well as our cultural and societal biases about the benefits, or evils, of wealth. Add to that our deep-seated personal fears regarding security, our often irrational or childlike concerns about being cared for and valued, and you've got an emotionally charged topic indeed.

And that's just for traditional couples. Add role reversal to the mix and conflicted feelings become exponential. *His* feelings about the very real loss of the control, like, say, when he's asking his wife for his grocery allowance. Or how about *her* feelings that she is somehow less feminine because she's earning the money instead of letting him take care of her and the family? It can make you crazy if you're not careful.

So, let's see if we can get your feelings about money out on the table with the following money matters quiz.

The Money Matters Quiz

You're going to take this quiz twice, so get a couple of blank sheets of paper and be ready to answer the following questions as honestly as you can. Answer once for yourself and then again as you think your spouse would answer the questions. Only, don't identify which answer sheet is which—because when you're finished, you and your partner are going to trade answer sheets to see if you can get a better handle on each other's feelings about emotional finance.

So, here goes. For each question, rank your answers 1 through 10; 1 means you strongly disagree, 5 is somewhere in the middle, 10 means you strongly agree. Then take the quiz all over again, answering as you think your partner would. Swap answers and discuss your results. You'll probably be amazed to find out how your spouse *really* feels about role-reversed money matters.

Rank from 1 to 10 (1: strongly disagree; 10: strongly agree):

1. She is uncomfortable or resentful at being the primary wage earner.
2. She enjoys being the wage earner because it makes her feel powerful.
3. A part of her doesn't respect him because he earns little or no money.
4. She feels more entitled to spend money on herself because she's the breadwinner.
5. She misses being "treated" to such things as dinners out

and small gifts and wishes she weren't always the one to
have to pay.

6. With friends, relatives, and co-workers, she is embarrassed
that she earns the money in the family.

7. She worries that she'll always be the primary provider and
that he will never be able to earn a substantial living.

8. She considers the marriage a 50–50 financial partnership—
it's not *her* money, it's *our* money.

9. A part of him resents her because she's the breadwinner.

10. Although she is the primary wage-earner, he likes to feel
financially in control by paying the bills, picking up the
check in restaurants, handling the budget, and so on.

11. He feels less entitled to spend money on himself because
he's not earning it.

12. He has a hard time asking her for money because it feels
like a blow to his pride.

13. He feels that his job as at-home dad is worth as much as
the income she earns from her job.

14. He doesn't like receiving an "allowance" from his wife—it
makes him feel inferior or subservient.

15. He doesn't judge his worth by financial standards.

16. He feels fine about not earning an income, but is still
embarrassed to admit this to friends and relatives.

17. We communicate very well about money matters.

18. We tend to avoid talking about money matters because it
brings up unresolved emotional issues.

19. We would probably have fewer conflicts over money if we
both had an income.

20. We fight about money but we never get to the underlying
emotional issues.

Now, swap papers and have at it. What did this bring up for
you? Were you surprised by your own emotions and by your
spouse's? This is the time for each of you to get your financial feelings out on the table. If necessary, discuss any lingering conflicts
or residual resentments before moving on. Then let's talk about

some ways you might be able to adjust your financial behavior so that you and your spouse can consider money for what it is—cash to live on—rather than imbuing it with all kinds of emotional meaning.

Control. Who's really holding the financial reins, and what kinds of changes, if any, do you want to make? Just because she's the primary breadwinner doesn't mean she should make all the financial decisions. And the split doesn't have to be 50–50. Decide how you're going to divvy up the fiscal responsibilities so that you both have some sense of power and control. Maybe he does the long-term financial planning, but she pays the bills. Or he does the day-to-day budgeting, but she handles the investments.

Sensitivity. Working wives need to be mindful of their at-home guy's feelings when it's time to pay the bill or tip the bell-man. Whatever makes him feel like he's in charge, make sure you let that happen when it's appropriate. Even if you play the power broker at work, closing million-dollar deals all day long, don't fight him for the check at dinner. After all, he earned the money as squarely as you did, by keeping the home fires burning so that you could be free to wheel and deal.

Bank Accounts and Credit Cards. Decide who's going to do the banking in your family and how you will set up your accounts. Do you need two checking accounts so you don't trip each other up and you both feel that you have a little flexibility and freedom? Can you live with a joint household account and separate credit cards? Discuss the possibilities and decide on a mutually workable plan.

Allowance. At-home dads are grown hardworking men. So, working moms, take some care when you're doling out the cash. Decide together how you're going to handle the household budget and don't make your husband feel like your six-year-old who gets fifty cents for his piggybank on Saturdays.

Appreciation. Most important of all, don't forget that you're a team here. Neither of you could be doing what you're doing if you didn't have each other. You're yin and yang, north and south, Burns and Allen, remember? So respect the fact that you each have a full-time job, one at home and one at work, and appreciate your partner every single day.

By now, we've seen that the SAHD/WM budgeting process involves a lot more than just juggling money. How you allocate your hard-earned dollars can mean the difference between a full-time parent being able to stay home with the kids, and both parents working full-time and turning the caregiver duties over to a third party. Most important, we've seen that it's not as hard as you might have imagined to live on one income. And, of course, the rewards to the family surpass anything mere money could buy.

We've also begun to understand the meaning of "emotional finance" and just how important sensitivity to this issue is for couples, especially role-reversed ones. So let's take an even closer look at some charged emotional issues as we discuss stereotypes.

Quick Review

Let's review what we've learned about finances with regard to feelings, as well as dollars and cents.

Sometimes one income is better than two.

Most two-career couples don't realize how much of their second income is eaten up by childcare and work-related costs. Once you look at your expenses, you may discover that you're not bringing home nearly as much as you think.

Do the math in three easy steps.

No matter what your current provider/caregiver family structure, it always makes sense to review your finances on some kind of regular schedule. Use the tables provided to figure out what you would earn as a two-career couple and as a one-income family. Then determine your family's monthly budget and compare.

Downsizing isn't as hard as you think.

If you've decided to give one-income living a go, you may want to look at the downsizing tips in this chapter to learn some easy ways to stretch your dollar. And even if you're still committed to two paychecks, it never hurts to learn a few money-saving budget boosters.

Don't ignore the emotional side of finance.

Make sure you and your spouse discuss the emotions surrounding financial issues. Recognize that your feelings about personal power, control, self-worth, and security can be all wrapped up in your earning power. Use the Money Matters Quiz to get your feelings out on the table and build ongoing dialogue about emotional finance.

Chapter 5

Mr. Mom &
Ms. Breadwinner

Overcoming the Stereotypes

David, at-home dad to two-year-old Jack and four-year-old Jenna, recalls an occasion when he was running errands one weekday morning. Standing on line at the bank, David was trying desperately to get his two fidgety kids under control long enough to cash a check. Finally, he turned to the youngsters and said, in no uncertain terms, "This is unacceptable. You're both driving me nuts today!" The woman in line behind him responded, "I'll bet you'll be happy to get back to the office." "Ma'am," David replied with all the dignity he could muster, "they are my office."

Debunking the Myths of Mr. Mom

O f all the relationship puzzle pieces that need to fit together before a couple is comfortable attempting a SAHD/WM role reversal, one of the trickiest is knowing that you may never completely escape the stereotypes. Be prepared to face some prejudices, but take comfort in the fact that it's nothing you can't handle. After all, just look how far you've come already. And if you've decided that a role-reversed parenting structure is best for your family, you're not going to let a little thing like a negative stereotype stop you from doing what you know is right, are you? Just as David attempted to take on the stereotypical attitude he encountered from the lady at the bank with a polite—okay, an *icily* polite—response, there are some simple solutions for combating prejudice. So let's take a little time out to investigate the most common at-home dad and working mom myths and some methods for counteracting them peacefully.

Myth #1: He's a Bumbling Mr. Mom

First, let's look at the most common, and also most painful, at-home-dad stereotype of them all. You know the one: the dopey "Mr. Mom" image from the Michael Keaton movie that gave an entire generation of stay-home dads a bad rap. Okay, maybe not completely. Michael Keaton's character loved his kids and eventually learned to handle the responsibilities of home and childcare, but he still came across as a buffoon bluffing his way from play dates to pediatricians.

There's only one way to tackle this one—and that's with good old-fashioned competence. There's nothing more effective for knocking off a stereotype and building a sense of confidence for the new at-home dad than discovering that he can, in fact, change a diaper and cook a meal—without dropping the baby or setting the kitchen on fire. Experience is an incredible teacher; SAHDs report a real sense of achievement and satisfaction at simply being able to handle things.

That's not to say that these dads aren't going to make mistakes. In fact, SAHDs expecting perfection are just victims in search of a trap into which to fall. So get over it, dads, you're not going to learn how to take care of kids and house overnight. These are acquired skills that millions of women had to learn long before you ever came along, and—big secret—some never got very good at them at all. But if you feel you need some advanced lessons or a crash course in at-home daddyhood, there are plenty of proactive things you can do.

Method: Fight Back with Competence. Just as you would in any other job, build up your skill set. Learn to cook, pick up some household cleaning tips, brush up on kidcare techniques, take an infant/child CPR or first aid class. Do whatever you need to do in order to feel competent and capable, including the time-honored tradition of calling on your mother or the stay-at-home mom next-door.

Time will always be an issue, so prioritize and get creative. And be sure to check out Chapter 10, "Tips from the Trenches," for a comprehensive list of kidcare and homecare strategies, but here are a few just to get you started.

Cooking

- If cooking's not your thing and you're getting tired of nuked nutrition, start with a basic cookbook like *Joy of Cooking* or *Cooking for Dummies*, an easy series like *365 Ways to Cook Chicken* and *365 Ways to Cook Pasta*, or a new favorite, Mark Bittman's *How to Cook Everything: Simple Recipes for Great Food*. Better yet, try getting a few kids' cookbooks for some easy how-to instructions. Most children's cookbooks have simple recipes with healthful ingredients and not too many of them. Your kids might even be inspired to help out if they see you using a book meant for them.
- The Food Network is another great source for fast, fun cooking tips. Try *The Naked Chef* ("naked" refers to healthy food, not the cook's state of undress) for some easy, irreverent cooking lessons.
- Don't overlook your local paper or pennysaver for recipes that aren't too challenging. And women's magazines—the downscale variety, not the gourmet food and wine mags—also have great, easy-to-use recipes and menus.
- Of course, there are always those old standbys, that is, the

recipes from the backs of boxes, cans, and jars just like Mom used to use.

Parenting Skills

- Again, be sure to subscribe to your free local newspaper for great ideas on childcare and also on workshops and seminars in your city. They often offer a Q&A with great advice and tips, frequently written by a doctor in your locale. Also be sure to check for kid-oriented activities and weekend festivals for families.
- Check out magazines like *Parents*, *Parenting*, and *Child*, and books like *What to Expect the First Year*. and the classic *Dr. Spock's Baby and Child Care*.
- Refer to the Resource Guide in the back of this book for more SAHD and parent-related websites, publications, and organizations.

Housekeeping

- If you're not hiring professional help, you'll have to learn the basics. Check Chapter 10 for the full list, but don't forget to consult your mother, mother-in-law, or "Hints from Heloise" or *Home Comforts: The Art and Science of Keeping House* by Cheryl Mendelsohn.

Myth #2: He Must Be a Loser

This one can really hurt. Some people, including your friends and neighbors, her colleagues, even your own relatives, may assume that you're staying home because you're financially incompetent or, even worse, some kind of slacker who refuses to take care of his family. That's why your wife has to go to the office every day and slave away to make ends meet while you're on the couch watching soaps all afternoon. Both of you, and even your kids if they're old enough, know it isn't so, but that doesn't make you feel much better when some Neanderthal slings an insulting comment your way.

Method: Think "Sticks and Stones." Remember the advice you gave your kids when some playground bully said something snotty to them? "Sticks and stones will break my bones but words will never hurt me," right? Well, try taking your own advice. Sure, it doesn't make you feel much better—same as your kid—but there's really not a lot you can do about the unenlightened's lack of enlightenment. Except, of course, to enlighten them. Try explaining your unique relationship to the uninitiated and see if you can get through. You won't always be able to, but once in a while you'll see a glimmer of understanding and newfound respect in the eyes of the video store manager who finally gets that you're a loving, involved father who's home in the middle of the day because he's taking care of his kids—on purpose.

Keep in mind that sometimes the biggest perpetuator of the "He must be a loser" myth can be the at-home dad himself. As you already know, it's usually not an easy decision to swap gender places, and once you've made it, it's still not an easy life to live. So, dads, if you're feeling conflicted about your role and finding ways to undermine your own position, consider getting some help. Talk to a counselor or a religious practitioner, or find a dads' group (check the Resource Guide at the back of this book) to give you some guidance. Most of all, don't keep your fears and doubts from your spouse, because you're in this together. If it doesn't work for both of you, it doesn't work.

Myth #3: He's a Wimp—or Worse

This is an adjunct to the "He must not be able to hold down a job" myth. This particular misconception takes the previous myth even deeper by suggesting that "this guy is a wimp with a wife who pushes him around" or "some kind of weirdo hanging around Gymboree all day." Granted, these seem a little extreme, but ask any stay-at-home dad who's ever tried to infiltrate a neighborhood playgroup run by at-home moms. It ain't easy. Many SAHDs say they feel like the human equivalent of the "What's wrong with this picture" that you see in kids' books. And it doesn't help when the moms give him a suspicious once-over or a good grilling about why, exactly, he's in the park at eleven a.m. with a toddler. After a while, though, even the most aloof of neighbor moms can turn into lifelong friends.

Method: Meet the Moms. There's only one way to strike back at this one—head-on, with as much personality as you can muster. Dads, you've got to get to know your comrades in arms, the at-home moms in your community. It's only through familiarity that they'll become comfortable and, even more important, accepting of you. And don't be passive about this. Reach out. Ask them to bring the stroller and meet you at Starbucks, get acquainted on the playground, invite their kids over to play in your backyard. In fact, you should shamelessly exploit your children as icebreakers and conversation starters. They'll thank you for it when they have a circle of buddies right on their block.

Most at-home moms are not used to having a strange guy around their little kids, and, let's be honest, any stranger gives every parent cause for concern. That is, until they get to know you and come to understand that you're home for exactly the same reason that they are. Because you love your kids and you value their well-being above all else, including your own career. So use your old networking skills (remember those?) and get out there and start meeting your new colleagues. Be friendly, be helpful, volunteer at school or on field trips. You may find you actually have a support system right in your own backyard. As one dad put it after he broke through the initially chilly facade and found friends among the moms, "I felt as though I'd walked among the apes and they accepted me." Okay, so maybe he stole that line from Dian Fossey, but you get the picture.

Just make sure that as you're getting to know the at-home mom, you're careful about your body language, level of familiarity, and physical contact. The last thing you want to do is to give her—

or her husband—the impression that you're hitting on her. Some SAHDs say that they've broken off relationships with at-home mom friends because the moms' working husbands were uncomfortable with their friendship. Other SAHDs suggest getting to know the couple—as a couple—before striking up a friendship with the at-home mom. Many of them do this by inviting the whole family over on a Saturday so, while the kids are playing, the guys and moms can bond separately and build trusting relationships, before the at-homers deepen their friendship.

Combating the Myths of the Overextended Breadwinner Wife

So we've seen a little of what the dads face on the domestic front. It can be a blow to the ego to fight for the acceptance, but most SAHDs have found that if they get out there and kiss babies and shake hands—just like an old-time politician—people will eventually see them for who they are and come to respect the sacrifices they've made for their constituents, er, families.

While at-home dads may face a public relations and perception problem, one that can be overcome by sheer resolve and diplomacy, the working wife may need to confront stereotypes that, if left unchecked, can be harmful. Because the prejudice that occurs on the job can affect opportunity, advancement, and, ultimately, her paycheck.

Myth #1: She Can't Be a Good Employee Because She's Got Kids

Wow! This one is so multilayered it can really do a number on an already stressed-out working mom. And, like most stereotypes, it has a kernel of truth that, if she's not careful, the mom may allow to feed her ever-present sense of guilt, a given according to virtually every working mom interviewed for this book.

This particular working-mom myth can come in many forms

and from all directions within the workplace. It can come from the competitive co-worker who volunteers to the boss, "Bridget always has to leave at five to get home to her kids, but I'm willing to put in the extra time needed to get the project done right." Or the supervisor who reports to management that "Laura would have been a good candidate for the promotion, but I couldn't expect her to travel or take on additional responsibility. Not with her kids at home." Now here's the worst part. Everyone else gets to look so noble and compassionate when it comes to you and your children, even while they're putting that last nail in your professional coffin.

And it's not that those assessments are necessarily inaccurate, it's that they aren't always relevant given your very stable childcare situation. Assuming Bridget and Laura were right for those jobs, shouldn't they at least have been given the opportunity? And let's not forget the big double standard at work here. Would any working father be passed over simply because he had kids at home? Particularly if his wife were home full-time parenting those kids? I don't think so.

Method: Prove 'Em Wrong. Lesson one for working moms— first, last and always: do not, repeat, do not apologize for having children. Don't apologize for having them, don't apologize for loving them, and don't apologize for putting their welfare before your employer's—or anyone else's, for that matter.

Now, that said, you do need to put your boss's mind at ease as to just what your dual commitments to your children and your job mean and how you plan to juggle them. Because they'll be nervous. Very nervous. In fact, the more necessary and irreplaceable you are, the more nervous your employer will be. But that doesn't have to be a bad thing. As long as you are in control of their fears and doubts and you clearly communicate your action plan to them.

Even though it's illegal for an employer to discriminate against you in the hiring phase for having children—they can't even ask you at the job interview—it's nearly impossible to keep your kids a secret once you're on the job. And why would you want to? Remember, *we're not apologizing for having a family*. But you may want to voluntarily explain your childcare situation to your boss in a positive and constructive light, especially if there are any factors that could directly affect your job duties or your co-workers. You want "buy-in." That is, you want to present a solution, not a problem, and to get your colleagues on board and supporting your efforts right from the beginning.

Explain how important your kids are—that's why your husband is home with them full-time—and how important your job is—that's why you've arranged your life so you're not worrying constantly or rushing out the door to pick them up at daycare every night at five. Demonstrate how committed you are to your job and your family. Then make sure you walk the walk. Put in the extra hours when you're needed, cover a co-worker's shift when you can, bring your husband and kids by to meet the boss if it's appropriate and welcome in your workplace. Let people know that these are living, breathing human beings, and they're important to you, just as your job is. And the commitment, care, and dedication that you show your family are exactly what make you a team player and a great employee for the long haul!

Myth #2: She Can't Be a Good Mom Because She's Got a Job

Working fathers seem to have escaped this one. Men who devote long hours and endless energy to their jobs are viewed as responsible and dedicated to their careers and to their families. Their families are the reason they're working those long hours in the first place, right? But somehow, if women devote the same time and energy to their jobs they are viewed with suspicion. There's a glitch in people's brains that makes them peg these moms as cold, calculating, or uncaring. In other words, if they're good businesswomen, they must not really be able to love small, needy, helpless human beings. Hmmm.

You've probably heard some variation on this theme: "What kind of mother is she? She's never home." "You mean she actually goes on business trips and leaves her kids at home?" Even the relatively harmless "She works way too hard" from her mother or best friend can sting. There's usually no acknowledgment that the kids are home safe and sound with Dad, a loving full-time parent, who has decided to stay home not only so he can be with the kids, but also so that his wife can succeed in her career.

But just like the dads who fall into the "He must be a loser" trap, there are plenty of working wives who sign themselves up for the "I must be a lousy mother" club. The admission price is guilt and the monthly dues are ongoing stress. Do yourself a favor and don't join it. And don't forget, just like the moms we met in Chapter 2 who actually prefer working outside the home and are woman enough to admit it, not every mom is the best candidate for stay-at-homedom. If that's why you're working and he's at home, lucky you. Aren't you the smart ones to have figured that out? Now, how about giving yourself a break and enjoying the role that you chose, by design, in full consciousness, with your husband's desire and consent? You both win—and so do the kids.

Myth #3: They Must Be the Weirdest Couple in the Neighborhood

This might, just possibly, be true. That is, if you think living your life and structuring your family the way you want it is weird. He may very well be the only stay-at-home dad in the neighborhood, or even the entire community. And she may be the only working wife married to an at-home dad in her company. Their own families might not know what to think of them.

Method: Rejoice in Your Role Reversal. So you're not just like the rest of the couples in your neighborhood. Congratulations. You're originals and you have the courage of your childcare convictions. And you are certainly not alone. In fact, your ranks are growing steadily. Now go fight the good fight!

Media Mania

Once again, we're going to point fingers at the media for perpetuating all these myths and negative stereotypes, right? Not exactly. Though we won't jump on the "Blame the media for the ills of the world" bandwagon, it wouldn't be fair to let them off the hook entirely either. Let's take a look at how realistically the infotainment world has portrayed families, and more specifically parents, over the years.

Just for fun, check out the list of sitcom families outlined below and see how they compare to their real-life counterparts by rating them on a 1–10 reality scale, then by seeing if you can spot your own family somewhere in the mix. Don't laugh—okay, laugh a little—but remember, these are all archetypes. Maybe not the ones Jung wrote about, but archetypes nonetheless. And if you buy into the notion that stereotypes spring from some sort of reality base, then you're sure to see yourselves, your family, or your friends in these scenarios. Think about it. Was your mom more of a Peg Bundy or a Harriet Nelson? Was dad an Ozzie Nelson or perhaps a Homer Simpson? And if you've never heard of any of these families, you're obviously not watching enough Nick at Nite. Just ask your kids; if they're old enough to have outgrown *Sesame Street*, they'll know.

Rate the parents on the following list on a scale of 1 to 10, 1 being least realistic, 10 being most realistic. Also check them out for stereotypes, negative and positive (that is, if you can find any positive ones . . .). Then pick out the couples and/or families that most resemble the one you grew up in and the one you've created with your spouse.

Write down your answers and ask your partner to do the same. Then compare notes and see if you had the same take on family styles and whether or not you hit on similar stereotypes. It may seem silly, but it's also very revealing and will definitely get you thinking and talking about the evolutionary process of building a family.

The TV Families Stereotype Quiz

Ozzie and Harriet (1950s)

The Nelsons represent the traditional family unit. The kind with two parents, a dad who works (though, in Ozzie's case, he never seemed to go anywhere) and a mom who takes care of the house, kids, and dog.

My Three Sons (1960s)

This is the single-father household, where dad struggles to raise his three boys, with plenty of male help from assorted grandfathers and uncles. For some unfathomable reason, this type of family structure became the norm for a slew of motherless television families for several decades.

One Day at a Time (1970s)

The flipside of *My Three Sons*, this is the single-mom scenario. Mom works full-time outside the home, struggles to raise her two girls, although the two teens do a decent job taking care of themselves, with no discernable help from anyone (except the gruff but wise building super).

Roseanne (1980s)

A blue-collar family where Dad worked outside the home, Mom took care of the kids until economics forced her to get a second job, and both parents struggled to raise their kids and make ends meet. Unlike the other sitcom moms, this one made no pretense of being a cook, glamour queen, or role model of any kind.

Married . . . with Children (1990s)

You remember Peg and Al? The dark—and funny—side of the traditional working dad/at-home mom couple. He moaned about how much he hated kids and marriage as he trudged off to his job at the shoestore. She wore Spandex (back when it wasn't cool), smoked cigarettes, and watched TV all day long. They had two kids from hell who were pretty much left to fend for themselves.

The Simpsons (cartoon time)

The most dysfunctional family on television, bar none, a classic for ten years and counting. Two cartoon parents, three demanding kids, and a quirky, crazy world swirling around them. A core of love covered with extreme nuttiness.

Okay, so some of this is just in fun as well as an attempt to look at the stereotypes about families that television has helped perpetuate over the years. Although as much as our society loves to blame the media for creating these images, they more likely mirror the stereotypes that we create ourselves. One thing is clear: few real families actually resembled these *traditional* TV families.

Even back when Ozzie and Harriet and the Cleavers set the standard for the supposed traditional American family, few parents could actually live up to those rosy images. Still, we grew up with an idealized vision of the mom in her apron and high heels vacuuming the kitchen (did your mom *ever* do that?) and the happy, hardworking dad grabbing his briefcase or lunch pail as he headed for the door, ready to do battle in the men's world of work.

Many still cling to this myth of the ideal traditional family, knowing full well that it's both unrealistic and outdated. But somehow it is what we have become accustomed to characterizing as traditional. Or normal. Or acceptable. The truth is, of course, that there are lots of types of families. Far more than the stereotypical sitcom families listed above. All equally acceptable, though arguably not all are very traditional. And if we have evolved to the point that we are capable of creating an Oreo that can turn our dunking milk bright blue, surely we've evolved enough to allow ourselves the freedom to explore options that will lead us to a family structure uniquely right for us.

From a Media Man

Los Angeles Times reporter and columnist Brian Lowry doesn't lend much credence to the ill effects of the media's family stereotypes. "I think that TV, with a few exceptions, is always behind the curve in chronicling shifts and attitudes." He believes that the shows don't form our beliefs—or illusions—so much as reflect and institutionalize them. In other words, once SAHDs had become an accepted part of public reality, *Mr. Mom* as well as the short-lived TV series *Daddio* were bound to follow.

Although *Daddio* was well received by a number of SAHDs, Lowry comments, "The whole joke is the guy has to stay home and take care of his kids, and that isn't really outlandish anymore. When *Mr. Mom* came out [in 1983], there was a certain novelty." Lowry emphasizes that this type of programming is about entertainment, not reality. What we see on the tube will always be heightened, skewed, or exaggerated to get the laughs—or the tears. For a more accurate picture of a social situation, "news magazines, like *20/20* and *Dateline NBC*, are more defining than sitcoms or dramas."

Lowry mentions a few old favorites that, for him, found the balance between truth and entertainment: "*Home Improvement*, *Roseanne* in its early years, and the first *Cosby* series did it with the parent-kid issues. Just the silly things struck a nerve." But no matter how much real-life SAHDs might like shows that mirror the facts of their real lives, Lowry says, "Ultimately, the producer goes with what's working for audiences."

Stereotypes, Television, and Us

Okay, so maybe the sitcoms are not terribly damaging to non-traditional families. And there has been progress. In shows like *Bachelor Father*, *My Three Sons*, and *The Courtship of Eddie's Father*, mothers had to lie down and die before the paternal figure helped with the kids. In *Daddio*, at least Mom was alive and working. But does that mean we should discount the influence of media on our perceptions? Read these statistics and see what you think:

- Ninety-eight percent of American homes have at least one television and 86 percent have a VCR.

- In the typical home, the set is on more than seven hours a day.
- Kids ages 2–17 average 21½ hours of television watching per week.
- By the age of sixty-five, the average person will have watched nine years of television.

While specific shows with comedy-driven stereotypes may not rock our psychological boats, the constant, pervasive presence of turned-on televisions in our homes could amount to a kind of brainwashing. Perhaps that's where the battle is. Look at *these* numbers:

- Between age two and age eleven, kids watch more than 20,000 television ads a year.

That's 150 to 200 hours of commercials alone! According to 1998 research, gender identity and a sense of gender role in tasks begin for our kids in the preschool years. What does all this advertising teach the little ones about what it means to be male and female?

Are Boys Really Better, Freer, and More Plentiful?

Advertisers prefer to use boys in commercials, even when their products are unisex. These commercials either show boy and girl models together, or boys only. In commercials featuring *only* boy models, you'll see the boys in the street, in the yard, in the mall, on their scooters. In the girl-only commercials, you'll find the girl models safe at home. Boys are generally the only gender ever pictured in antisocial behavior (i.e., bad manners, breaking rules or objects, etc.). Girls almost always behave in a socially acceptable manner.

Once again, there has been *some* progress. Not that we need to see young girls engaging in negative or destructive behaviors just so we can even the score. But we are beginning to get beyond the images of passive girls who just sit there acting, well, girly. Now girls in commercials are sometimes allowed to be active, and occasionally we actually see them engaging in physical activity like athletics or dance. Finally, it seems, some advertisers are not sitting still for girls always sitting still.

In a landmark Kaiser Foundation Report, Nancy Signiorelli, a professor of communication at the University of Delaware, ran a study of the media most watched and read by adolescent girls, including commercials, television, films, magazines, music videos, and print advertisements. The good news is that she and her team did find a number of positive female role models who were intelligent and independent. But the overriding message in every medium is that girls and women focus on romance, dating, and how they look, while men focus on their jobs. Scary in this day and age, isn't it, that things haven't really changed all that much?

As far as representation in all these media—with the exception of magazines for teenaged girls—Signiorelli found females trailing sadly:

- TV shows featured only 45 percent female characters but 55 percent male characters.
- TV commercials featured 42 percent female characters, 58 percent male characters.
- Movies showed 37 percent female characters, 63 percent male characters.
- Only 22 percent of music videos showcased female performers (as opposed to the millions of scantily clad, look-alike nymphets dancing around the performers), but 78 percent featured male performers.

Ergo . . . at the root of the media's family stereotypes are the same old tired gender stereotypes against which we have fought for so long. From the cited statistics, we see that we can't turn to the media for support or guidance, since they're *waaaaay* behind us on the evolutionary chain. So what can we do?

We can be more aware of our children's exposure to arthritic

and irrelevant sexual clichés. We can encourage them in their indi-
viduality and independent thinking. We can show more confidence and pride in our nontraditionalness and express our pleasure
in the payoffs. We can remind our kids—and ourselves—not to
accept as reality everything we see in ads, read in magazines, or
watch on a screen.

Nothing is more powerful than the truth of a direct experience.
If Dad at home and Mom on the job make your family happier,
healthier, and stronger, you, your kids, and the world will know.
Our best defense against societal stereotypes and media myths is
our own living, breathing everyday example.

Quick Review

Concerns about stereotypes, both male and female, can sometimes be intimidating to couples who are attempting to redefine
traditional roles, especially in the beginning. But they don't have
to stop you from doing what you know is right for your family.

***Once you recognize the SAHD/WM myths,
it's time to try these methods for counteracting
them effectively.***

Myths and Methods—His

- *Myth #1:* He's a dopey Mr. Mom bumbling his way through
  home and childcare.
  Method: Fight back with competence and brush up on your
  skills in caregiving, cooking, and housekeeping.
- *Myth #2:* He must be a loser if he's living off his wife.
  Method: If you feel you could fall prey to this one, investigate
  your own feelings about your role then take action, including
  seeking professional help or support from other SAHDs.
- *Myth #3:* He's some kind of weirdo who can't hold down a
  job or fit in with the grownups.

Method: Get to know the moms in your neighborhood. They can be your biggest allies and supporters.

Myths and Methods—Hers

- *Myth #1:* She can't be a good worker because she's got kids.
  Method: Educate your boss and colleagues that dedication to your job and dedication to your family don't have to be mutually exclusive, especially when you have a full-time parent at home.
- *Myth #2:* She must not be a very good mom because she's got a job.
  Method: While this one is so subtle it can be hard to combat, you can simply refuse to give in to it.
- *Myth #3:* They sure are a weird couple.
  Method: Embrace your uniqueness and make it work for you.

We may not be able to blame the media for creating negative stereotypes, but we should be aware that they sometimes perpetuate them.

Just for fun, take this TV Families Stereotype Quiz to see if your family is anything like the families we've grown up watching on television.

Studies show that the media continues to treat men and women differently, but then that's really no surprise, is it? Just be aware that the most important defense against stereotypes is the daily example we set for our children.

Chapter 6

Dad and Mom Parenting Styles—and the Kids Who Benefit from Both

"Dad generally changes a diaper 30 to 40 percent faster than Mom. He does this with brute strength, grabbing both ankles in one hand, partially inverting the toddler and keeping him in the ideal position for a one-handed fast wipe and new diaper. If moms try this, it's just plain scary. The kid ends up twisting around in the poopy diaper, never properly clearing the tooshie area, and it's a mess. This is a daddy technique that moms should never attempt unsupervised."

Strong words of advice from Mitch, a stay-at-home dad full of tips from the trenches. Besides being a great diapering tip, Mitch's unique inversion technique is a perfect example of how moms and dads parent differently. No statistic-citing expert could possibly have painted a more vivid picture.

We've already looked at male/female stereotypes and seen how men and women are treated differently by others. In this chapter, we'll take a closer look at some actual, rather than perceived, differences. We'll find out how moms and dads utilize distinct parenting styles and, most important, how the kids can benefit from both. We'll also hear directly from the children in SAHD/WM families to find out how they feel about being parented by both Mom and Dad—and about having Dad as the at-home parent.

Different but Equal

Jenny is the twelve-year-old daughter of at-home dad Blake and working mom Alison. Although Jenny loves having Dad take care of her, when it comes to homework, Jenny says lately she'd rather have Mom in charge. "Sometimes Dad just refuses to help me. 'Figure it out,' he usually tells me when I can't do something. He won't even let me complain if I get frustrated. But Mom is much more patient. She'll sit down with me and listen to why I'm having so much trouble."

These approaches—Mom's comforting style and Dad's do-it-yourself technique—are fairly typical of the way men and women parent. Obviously, we'll be talking about generalizations, and we all know parents who buck trends (especially role breakers like SAHD/WMs), but there are some broad patterns that men and women fall into, as both common sense and the childcare experts tell us. The significant thing here is that, if you combine the two approaches, the child gets the benefit of learning to cope with frustration—a must for the future risk takers of the world—but also a sense of operating from a secure, loving base.

But before we go any deeper into specific gender-related parenting styles, it's important to note that most experts agree that there is no predisposition for either gender to be a better parent. As the child development authority Michael Lamb states, "With the exception of lactation, there is no evidence that women are biologically predisposed to be better parents than men. Social convention, not biological imperatives, underlie the traditional division of parental responsibilities." In other words, neither Mom nor Dad has a corner on the childcare business. Both can be equally effective except for breastfeeding, which Mom pretty much owns. But equal does not mean the same. Society, individual parental personalities, even the personality of the child, all influence the way men and women parent.

Parenting in Mommy Mode or Daddy Style

Like marriages and snowflakes, no two mom and dad parenting styles are alike. Stereotypes—as well as some research—suggest women are more compassionate and affectionate, while men are more action- and task-oriented. Regardless of science or stereotypes, however, trend-setting stay-at-home dads and working moms seem to find their own balance. They do it their way. The motto we've heard from the most successful couples is "Whatever works, keep on doing it!" It's important to recognize your own style and that of your mate, so you can more effectively raise happy, caring, self-reliant kids. Let's take a look at some of these mom and dad parenting styles, and how they play out in the context of specific parenting issues.

Play, Nurturing, and Physical Mishaps

Child-and-father play is a critical part of raising children, affirms the Rutgers University scholar David Popenoe: "The way fathers play affects everything from the management of emotions to intelligence and academic achievement. It is particularly important in promoting the essential virtue of self-control." As he points out, "At play and in other realms, fathers tend to stress competition, challenge, initiative, risk taking and independence." That's certainly true in the case of the Knapp family's story.

Clayton has been a stay-at-home dad to his six-year-old son, Jimmy, since the boy's birth. Clayton's wife, Beth, is an office manager at a manufacturing supply company. While Beth sees herself as a nurturer, she understands that the responsibility for hugs and kisses often falls on Clayton's shoulders. Occasionally to her dismay, but often to her amusement, Beth notes that Clayton has adopted a nurturing style very different from her own. She recalls a sledding incident from the previous winter when Jimmy took a bad tumble off his toboggan that resulted in a black eye. Knowing that Beth would "have a cow" when they returned home, Clayton counseled Jimmy on what he should say to his mom. As predicted, Beth gasped when Jimmy entered the house. But when Jimmy said, with a schoolyard swagger, "You oughta see the other guy," Beth couldn't help but laugh. She understood that Clayton fostered his own special brand of humor to soften the cuts, scrapes, and bruises of Jimmy's life. While it would never be Beth's style, she recognized that it worked for Clayton—and, even more to the point, for Jimmy.

Unpredictability is also an often-predictable factor in fathering. According to Dr. Kyle D. Pruett's *Fatherneed*, infants between seven and thirteen months respond even more favorably to being picked up by Dad than by Mom. Moms more often pick up the baby for maintenance, while Dad picks up the infant because he senses that the child wants to play or, just as often, because *Dad* wants to play with the baby. And *how* Mom and Dad each pick up the infant can be just as different as *why* they pick him up. In most of the world, moms tend to carry babies facing toward their own bodies, often so they are free to breast-feed. Dads carry babies facing outward, with a view of the world, in what is known in this country and others as the football hold, itself an action description for an action-oriented parenting mode.

When eighteen-month-old Noah was an active toddler, his at-home dad, Michael, and working mom, Laura, used to argue constantly about Michael's laissez-faire approach to Noah's physical well-being. As Laura described it, "Michael and I used to do battle over allowing Noah to navigate our outside stairway by himself. Michael insisted that if Noah fell, it would be good experience! 'He'll learn how to fall,' he'd argue." But since Dad was a full-time at-home dad, Michael's rough-house style won out over Laura's more conventional approach. Noah, now an adventurous teenager, takes spills and tumbles—both physical and emotional—in stride.

Morality/Values

Candace was waiting on her neighbors' porch with her ten-year-old daughter, Susan, who was working on the annual candy sale for her class. Candace, a sales representative for a large linen manufacturer, had been traveling quite a bit in the last several weeks and wanted to spend this time with her daughter, while her husband, Bernie, was home starting dinner. As the neighbor graciously agreed to buy some chocolate, Candace noticed that her daughter was copying the order into her notebook in addition to filling out the required order form. Susan later explained that someone at the school had "messed up" some of the orders last year and that she was going to double-check her notes to make sure that she—and her customers—received exactly what they ordered.

Candace realized at that moment the profoundness of that piece of paper. Her daughter felt an obligation to their neighbors. She was being responsible and accountable. Neither Candace nor Bernie had ever lectured Susan on the importance of honesty and responsibility, yet she clearly had picked up on this by watching Candace deal with her customers. Later that night, Candace told Bernie about Susan's actions, recognizing how significant her own behavior had been in teaching their daughter the value of responsibility.

Watching her mother had imparted key values for Susan, but her interaction with her father may be at least as important. Child development experts note that men play an especially vital role in promoting the "soft" virtues such as compassion. David Popenoe, of Rutgers, says: "We don't often think of fathers as teachers of empathy, but involved fathers, it turns out, may be of special importance for the development of this character trait, essential to an ordered society of law-abiding, cooperative, and compassionate adults. Examining the results of a 26-year longitudinal study, a trio of researchers at McGill University reached a 'quite astonishing' conclusion (from *The Wilson Quarterly* Spring 1996, excerpted in *Utne Reader* October 1996). The single most important childhood factor in developing empathy is paternal involvement in childcare.

Fathers who spent time alone with their children more than twice a week—giving meals, baths, and other basic care—reared the most compassionate adults." Just imagine what a full-time at-home father could do!

Ed is a stay-at-home dad to six-year-old Ryan and ten-year-old Kyle. Working mom Gina is a human resources executive for a large company. Because Ed is home with the kids and in charge of both the family calendar and holiday planning, when the boys were old enough to participate, he decided that they would "adopt" a needy family for Christmas through their city's Chamber of Commerce. Now, every year for the holidays, Ed and the kids visit a different family and volunteer their services for household repairs, clean-up jobs and cosmetic fixes. Thanks to this empathetic and sensitive father, what began as a onetime charitable deed has evolved into an important family tradition and life lesson for Ryan and Kyle.

Discipline

The words "Wait until your mother gets home" will probably never be uttered by a stay-at-home dad (unless it's been a really, really bad day). Much as stay-at-home moms find themselves dishing out discipline on the spot, stay-at-home dads have discovered that correcting behaviors or preventing disasters requires immediate response. By the time the other parent arrives home hours later, the behavior is forgotten and the punishment no longer fits the crime. But as many parents discover, they often have different ideas of what is acceptable in setting boundaries for a child. When the subject is discipline, dads and moms both do it—just a bit differently.

Janice, a salon owner, spends Sundays and Mondays at home with her two-year-old, Jack, while at-home dad Steve cares for him the rest of the week. Cooking dinner one night, Janice had found she was constantly interrupted by the need to pull Jack away from the cookbook shelf. He was intent on pulling every cookbook down onto the floor and spreading the pile throughout the kitchen. Janice aired her frustration to Steve, only to discover that during the work week he not only allowed but encouraged Jack to pull the books down. In his view, it kept their active toddler occupied and out of danger while he cooked. This was clearly an instance where Janice and Steve were not on the same page.

Janice told Steve that she wanted to discourage this behavior. Steve felt just the opposite. Since the majority of the cooking fell on his shoulders, he wanted to let Jack play with the cookbooks. Janice suggested they compromise and move some of Jack's own children's books onto the shelves, but Steve said that he had tried that, and it had failed. Steve rationalized that the cookbooks they really loved already had grease marks and food stains on them, and the others were just taking up space anyway. What additional harm could Jack do? Janice relented. In the ensuing discussion, she discovered the couple had vastly different tolerance points for various toddler behaviors. If she and Steve hadn't had this discussion, innocent Jack would have been encouraged and reprimanded for the same action.

Fourteen-year-old Maya is an only child cared for by long-time at-home dad Charlie. Working mom Evie is a district superintendent for their local public school system. When Maya decided to stop swimming competitively, after competing since she was in kindergarten, her parents worried that she wouldn't get enough exercise in her daily routine. And, in fact, Maya suddenly seemed more interested in the telephone and computer than anything remotely resembling physical fitness. Charlie's solution was to help Maya find another sport or activity as soon as possible. He didn't care whether it was karate or kickboxing, as long as she got some regular exercise.

Evie had a slightly different approach. Her thought was that Maya would have to earn her phone and computer time through a "time bank" system. So many hours of physical exercise—as defined by Maya and her parents—would result in a certain number of hours of phone/computer time. They would track the time bank on a chart posted on the refrigerator, and Maya would be responsible for adding and deleting the appropriate number of hours.

Charlie thought Evie's approach was a little too complicated, while Evie thought Charlie's style was a bit too dictatorial. So they did what smart parents everywhere do—they involved Maya directly in the decision-making process. Naturally, she came up with exactly the right solution for the situation. Understanding that the underlying concern was that she wouldn't be getting enough exercise, Maya decided to try the time bank system, with a backup plan that if, in the course of building up her time bank account, she found a regular sport or form of fitness that could replace swimming, she'd drop the time bank. In the meantime, she and her parents determined time bank values for walking to and from school, biking with her dad, family hikes, and other physical activities. Eventually, Maya decided to try out for the basketball team, and the time bank became a thing of the past. But the experience proved that a shared approach to discipline could be extremely effective.

Chores

Different parenting styles play out in a big way over how chores are handled. Whether it's mess tolerance or checkbook balancing, what happens when one partner doesn't like the way the other partner is handling responsibilities? Can you teach an old dog new tricks, or does the old dog delegate, trading for a different trick?

Angelica, a legal secretary, and Peter, a former auto mechanic and stay-at-home dad to five-year-old Carter and seven-year-old Ruth, describe their travails when it comes to chores. Unlike his wife, Peter loves to drive, and now that the kids are in school, he finds he's always in the car. Peter calls it his mobile office. Poised with a mounted pen and paper, a car phone, and a "phat" stereo system, Peter is the master of errands and the king of the carpool. Ask Peter to boil some spaghetti, however, and you'll hear some angst-filled protestations.

Unfortunately Angelica's erratic schedule, and Peter's love of the road, and his fear of the kitchen, add up to some pretty unhealthy living. Carter and Ruth were being fed a constant diet of drive-through fast food. Angelica decided that her love of cooking could be passed on to Peter. Not so. Despite repeated attempts at Cooking 101, Peter failed miserably. He didn't enjoy cooking and never would. Though they had a housekeeper once a week (a compromise that they had made from the beginning), they didn't feel their budget could stretch to include a cook. It could, however, handle a chest-style freezer that fit in the garage. Once a month, Angelica spent the day cooking and freezing healthy meals that only needed to be popped into the microwave. She cooked big meals like her grandmother used to make. It satisfied her maternal urges, and she looked oh-so-Martha-Stewart in her apron.

Angelica and Peter felt that with this new system everything was on track—except their basement. "Don't even go down there. That's our next project." Sometimes being a parent means that a few things slide, for a little while at least, and then the kids are old enough to help clean them up.

No examination of chores would be complete without some focus on how parents actually get kids to help. From bribes to threats to rewards, Mom and Dad parenting styles once again come into play.

Working mom Vicki and at-home dad Jon routinely fought over two things when it came to their three kids: chores and allowance. It was only when Jon, out of sheer desperation, decided to combine the two, that the lightbulb went off. Although Vicki believed that an allowance should be given as a rite of passage, with rules for use spelled out, Jon felt strongly that an allowance was a privilege and should be earned by, you guessed it, doing chores.

As the responsibility of caring for a large house, three active kids, a dog, and twelve goldfish grew with each passing day, Jon finally put his foot down. He was home dealing with all this, Vicki spent long hours at her job (and sometimes out of town) as a computer systems consultant, and he felt he should have more say in what was required of the children as contributors to the household. Vicki agreed that Jon was entitled to set the ground rules, so he went to work. He assigned the kids, two boys and a girl aged eleven, nine, and four, specific age-appropriate chores. They would get an allowance every week, also tied to their ages, but only if all their chores had been completed. A checklist was posted in the kitchen. Since the three kids, unlike Maya, weren't old enough to take responsibility for their own posts, Jon oversaw the completion of the chores and their recording on the checklist.

At first resistant, the kids soon came to accept chores and checklists as daily routine. And every Sunday, part of the family's pre-church ritual was the recording of the chores, the handing out of the allowance, and thanks all around for jobs well done.

Learning. While both parents provide crucial influence, involved fathers may have more of an impact on a child's learning than we might think. According to research by several organizations, including the National Center for Fathering, fathers' involvement seems to be linked to the ability to deal with frustration, improved problem-solving ability, and higher academic achievement. Several studies have found that the presence of the father is one determinant of girls' proficiency in mathematics. And one pioneering study found that the amount of time fathers spent reading was a strong predictor of their daughters' verbal ability. This isn't to negate moms' role in helping with homework or fostering good learning habits, but it makes clear the responsibility that both parents have in their children's education.

Studies have also demonstrated a strong relationship between fathers' involvement and the quantitative and mathematical abilities, as well as verbal intelligence, of their sons. While Dad's and Mom's styles may differ, the key here is definitely ongoing, regular involvement in the child's learning. Learning, of course, doesn't just mean school or homework. Parents influence how their children feel about the *process* of learning, stimulating intellectual curiosity, expanding academic horizons, and encouraging kids to become life-long learners.

Melissa, an accounts payable supervisor for a large car rental agency, is married to Philip, who takes care of their nine-year-old son, Richard. Melissa and Philip are both avid readers who strongly believe in challenging their son intellectually and exposing him to a wide variety of cultural and academic pursuits. However, both parents grew more and more worried when, despite their encouragement, they noticed that Richard did not enjoy reading. His grades were adequate, he turned in his homework on time, and his teacher was not terribly concerned, at least not yet; but Melissa and Philip knew how important a love, or at least tolerance, of reading is to overall academic achievement. However, when it came to Richard and reading, that's all Philip and Melissa agreed on; they had very different views on how to rectify the situation. Philip felt that they should impose some very strict guidelines on Richard to get him to start reading more, including further reducing his already limited television, computer, and Nintendo time. Melissa heartily disagreed, saying that this was exactly the sort of approach that might turn Richard off reading forever.

Instead, Melissa instituted a Saturday afternoon ritual for mother and son. The two of them would go to the public library, check out a couple of books, then go out for lunch together. Sometimes they'd pick up a picnic and, with blanket, books, and sandwiches, spend a quiet afternoon in the park. Other times, they would take their books home and curl up on the couch to read, fortified with hot chocolate and cookies. Richard came to associate reading with pleasant, relaxed afternoons and, over time, the reading habit began to form. Both parents were gratified to notice that computer and television time naturally dwindled as Richard spent more time reading. And as an additional bonus, their reading ritual was a great way for Melissa and Richard to have more working mom–kid time together and for Philip to get Saturday afternoons to himself.

A Working Mom Should Respect the At-Home Dad's Routine

A common concern among at-home dads is that, because their wives feel out of touch with the children during the day, they'll come home at night and try to overcompensate by playing with the kids when it's not playtime. Or keep their kids awake past their bedtime, so that Mom can have some one-on-one time with them. But sleep deprivation can be damaging. Dr. Marc Weissbluth notes in his book *Healthy Sleep Habits, Happy Child*, "Don't think that it has no lasting effect when you routinely keep your child up too late—for your own pleasure after work or because you want to avoid bedtime confrontations . . . Cumulative, chronic sleep losses, even of brief duration, may be harmful for learning." Here's how several couples dealt with what, in reverse, is a classic mom-dad problem.

Doug's a stay-at-home dad to eleven-month-old Sean. "One thing that would drive me crazy was when Erin came home from work. She would want to play with Sean, which I understood, but she would hype him up when she should have been winding him down for bedtime." Erin just didn't understand that the bedtime ritual needed to start as soon as she walked in the door. She felt she was missing out entirely on playing with her son; weekends weren't enough. Finally, Erin and Doug found a compromise. Erin got up an hour earlier in the morning, rising when Sean awoke. She'd change him out of his pajamas, and then the two would play for an hour and eat breakfast together. This allowed for one-on-one mom-and-son time, without affecting Sean's bedtime wind-down. To avoid losing sleep, Erin went to bed earlier rather than watching her favorite TV dramas at night.

Stan, another at-home dad, says, "I feel like I have to be the voice of reason sometimes." Stan takes care of twin fourteen-year-old girls, Stephanie and Carrie. His wife, Yvette, is a federal prosecutor in a major metropolitan area. When Yvette came home after a long day in court, she just wanted to veg. The girls, who wanted to be with her, ended up watching movies or TV shows until after eleven on school nights. After a call from Stephanie's teacher that she had fallen asleep in class, Stan had to put his foot down for the whole family. "Stephanie and Carrie want Yvette's attention, but need her full attention. No one can compete with the television.

Everyone's in bed by ten or ten-thirty now. If a show is important, we tape it for weekend viewing, though it's usually relegated to the unwatched stack as other things become more important." Yvette realizes how much she relied on the TV to numb her from her day, when she really relished "talk time" with her daughters.

Dana is another working mom who has come up with a solution to the "not enough time with my kids" dilemma, without ruining Dad's carefully established routines. Obviously, with her husband Bob taking the stay-at-home parent role, most of the childcare responsibilities fall on his shoulders. Even though the role-reversed structure is working wonderfully with Barry, eight, and Ryan, six, Dana feels out-of-touch with her kids and guilty about it. To compensate, she makes sure that special occasions are her domain. Holiday decorations, costumes, planning, invitations, baking, and everything else "special" gets entered onto her Palm Pilot. "I have to feel connected in a mommy sort of way, and this works for all of us. Maybe working fathers don't have the same guilt, but when I'm at work, I'm thinking of my boys and feeling like I should be in two places at once. At least with special occasions, I take on the event and Bob stays the course with the daily stuff. He doesn't feel like he's being overburdened, and I appease my guilt and create annual traditions with my sons."

Common sense and childcare experts have told us for years that kids crave routine. Parents and kids everywhere would agree. When my sons, Harrison and Zachary, were babies, they were routinely put to bed with music and blankies. Those blankies, now ten and six like their owners, have seen better days, but have become important not just as part of the bedtime ritual, but as a symbol of the routines that anchor the household. Harrison no longer needs his blankie at night. But just knowing it's tucked away in his drawer, he says, makes him feel good.

Rituals and routines are an important part of family life; when Dad is the primary caregiver, it often falls to him to create and develop them. Moms must be mindful not to shake them up needlessly, especially as an attempt to compensate for their own guilt at not being there. As Harrison puts it, "Moms are great for cuddling. But dads are good for all the regular stuff, like cooking. And you don't really need to cuddle *all* day long."

As routines and rituals grow into the daily fiber of family life, parents need to be cognizant of just how powerful the structure they've built can become for their kids. Sam had been a stay-at-home dad since his first of two daughters was born. His wife, Jackie, was an account manager at a major advertising agency. "BC," as Sam and Jackie refer to life "Before Children," Sam had been a marketing director for a consumer products company. Now that their girls, twelve-year-old Kate and ten-year-old Emily, were in school all day, as well as participating in several after-school activities, Sam was contemplating a return to work.

Sam, Jackie, Kate, and Emily sat down to a family meeting to discuss Sam's plan. He explained that when he and Jackie had first decided upon their family structure, it had always included Sam returning to the workforce once they felt that the girls were old enough. Sam told the girls he was getting his résumé updated to start a job search. What happened next was unexpected. It became apparent that Kate and Emily were very upset by the idea of Sam not being there for them when they returned home from school. Kate asked about helping with homework or special projects. Emily wanted to know who would drop her, and her viola, at school every day. Even though they were becoming very independent young women, Kate and Emily obviously wanted their dad to be there for them, every day, just like he always had.

Based on their reactions, Sam and Jackie rethought their decision. Sam revised his plans and started taking a couple of classes in anticipation of starting a part-time home-based business. Sam and Jackie really listened to their kids. They weighed their own wishes against those of their children and responded. Sam was overwhelmed by the love his daughters had for him. Though the girls were preteens now, Sam and Jackie didn't lose sight of the fact that they still needed and wanted a full-time parent at home. And that parent was, and would continue to be, Dad.

Kids Thrive on Two Styles of Parenting

Dads may play more rough-and-tumble; moms may be more concerned with safety. Dads may make a game out of homework or adopt a "do it yourself" attitude; moms may take a more consoling approach. As you've learned in this chapter, there are a number of parenting issues that women and men tend to handle differently. Add to those differences your unique personalities and upbringings, and it's clear that you and your mate bring different qualities to your children's lives.

The important thing to remember is that kids need the love, attention, encouragement, discipline, and influence of both parents. The wonderful benefit of becoming a SAHD/WM family is that your children are assured of the sustained involvement of their dads—a priceless advantage that they will treasure their whole lives.

Quick Review

Understanding some inherent differences in mom versus dad parenting styles can help you recognize that, when it comes to caregiving, there is always more than one approach and that can be good news for kids.

Society, not biology, dictates the division of parenting responsibilities.

Most childcare experts agree that there is no gender predisposition to make either mom or dad a better parent. With the exception of breastfeeding, which mom obviously owns, both parents can be equally effective caregivers.

When it comes to dad and mom parenting styles, vive la différence.

Although neither Mom nor Dad is automatically the better parent just by virtue of their gender, there are some differences in male/female parenting. But rather than viewing those differences as a problem, you should think of them as a bonus. Kids get the benefit of dual perspectives on dealing with conflict resolution, risk-taking, values, discipline, even playtime and rough-housing. And though parents may agree on the end result in childrearing, the fact that they each have their own means of getting there just makes life richer.

Moms need to respect dads' routines.

Working moms may sometimes attempt to compensate for their away-from-home hours by bending dads' routines when they're in charge, especially when it comes to bedtime and discipline. "Not fair," say the stay-at-home dads. Moms need to honor the rules established by dad since he's the full-time caregiver. It may be easier said than done, but working moms must recognize that when they shake things up, it is often for their own emotional needs, not for the kids.

Chapter 7

Career Planning for the Role-Reversed Couple

Finding the Work-Family Balance

"I think you should set up the interview," at-home dad Marcus told his wife, Judy, one morning as she packed her bags for a business trip. *"It sounds like a great opportunity, and you're the one who always says, 'Take the meeting, you never know where it will lead.' "*

"I'm so overloaded now, I don't even know how I could squeeze a breakfast meeting onto my calendar at this point," responded Judy, a marketing exec for a financial services corporation. Stress was evident in her voice.

"But that's the whole point. Maybe another job would be less stressful and you wouldn't have to travel so much. If you could cut back on your hours, even a little, or build some flexibility into your schedule, then I could begin to look at some options for going back to work."

"You want to go back to work? Now?" Judy replied in horror, as though the thought had never crossed her mind. *"But Madison is only four! What if we decide to have another baby? What if . . ."*

I t's not easy being a one-income, role-reversed family. It's even harder to look ahead and plan for the future. But if Mom doesn't want to become a corporate slave and Dad doesn't plan to be chained to the washer and dryer for the rest of his natural life, then planning is the name of the game. That's what this chapter is all about, and it starts with finding the balance between your commitments to career and family. Of course, those commitments can co-exist harmoniously, but often as not, they can also contribute unnecessary conflict to your already chaotic household. Hey, you've got kids! Chaos is part of the deal, but let's try to keep it manageable and enjoyable chaos, shall we?

It's All About Balance

Balance is a process, not a destination. Like marriage and child-rearing, balance is fluid and ever-changing by its very nature. The specific type of balance we're talking about here is the one between work and home, which we can look at from a couple of different perspectives. First, let's look at the balance between Mom's and Dad's career goals. Admittedly, Mom's work may be the priority because she's the breadwinner, but that doesn't mean that Dad's career goals should be ignored forever. And the same logic holds on the home front. With Dad the at-home parent, his family issues take precedence, but Mom's family needs and goals should also be considered.

Just take a look at Judy and Marcus. Both have work–family issues that obviously need to be addressed. Clearly, Judy is unhappy with the amount of time she is spending at work and on the road. And Marcus seems to be harboring career goals that he has yet to articulate or negotiate with his wife. The good news is, they're talking about these issues *before* they become crises.

This chapter will give you some tools to help you examine the work–family balance in your lives and help you make the desired adjustments. But before you can take action and make the changes that will move you in the direction you wish to go, you need to have a clear idea of your goals.

What Are Your Career Goals and What Are Your Family Goals?

Before we can go any further with the concept of balancing work and family, we need to figure out what you and your spouse really want from your careers and from your family life. Let's start with a simple career–family balance assessment. You can do this separately, then discuss your responses. You can also answer as you think your partner might, then swap answers to see if you're really on target.

Working Mom Career–Family Balance Assessment

Answer True or False for each of the following.

1. I love getting up and going to work each day.
2. My work is as important to me as having a family.
3. I work because I have to.
4. I would like to work more.
5. I would like to work less.
6. I have additional career goals I would like to pursue while my husband is at home.
7. I would prefer to stay home and take care of the kids and house.
8. I feel guilty because I'm away from the kids so much.
9. I feel guilty because I like my job so much.
10. I would like more freedom on my job so I could attend more kid and family activities.
11. I would like to have a telecommuting position.
12. I feel I'm constantly shortchanging my family.
13. I feel I'm constantly shortchanging my job.
14. I feel I'm constantly shortchanging myself.
15. I would like to develop a home-based business.

At-Home Dad Career–Family Balance Assessment

Answer True or False for each of the following statements.

1. For now, I am perfectly content staying home with the kids.
2. I see myself staying home for less than five years.
3. I see myself as a SAHD for more than five years.
4. I miss going to work every day.
5. I'm a little fearful of getting back into the swing of work, since I've been away for a while.
6. I'd like to become a work-at-home dad.
7. I don't think my wife realizes how much I miss my work.
8. I'd like to figure out a plan to get me back to work as soon as possible.
9. I feel that life is passing me by since I've been home.
10. Being home with my kids has been the greatest time of my life.
11. I'm thrilled to support my wife's career efforts.
12. I'm sometimes jealous of my wife's career.
13. I'd like to switch places with my wife.
14. I could easily stay home until my kids are in college.
15. I worry that I no longer have any relevant job skills.

Now take a look at your answers and those of your spouse. Are you surprised by your own responses or those of your partner? What issues or emotions did your discussion bring up? Hang on to those feelings as we go a little deeper into career-planning mode. And why not make a note on your family business plan to retake this quiz the next time you sit down to reevaluate your job descriptions or, at least, at the end of each year?

Three-Step Career Planning: From Me to We

Angela and Bill thought they had the work–family thing all figured out. A recent business school graduate and mother of their nine-year-old boy and four-year-old girl, Angela planned to accept a position at a large accounting firm, then eventually start her own business as a financial planner. Bill, who was working full-time as a promotions manager at a local radio station when they were first married, had quit his job three years ago to take care of the kids while Angela worked full-time and went to grad school at night. He's now planning to launch a home-based promotion and marketing business.

Sounds like these two energetic and ambitious parents could have quite a lively partnership, right? Trouble was, they never really consulted each other on their individual goals and timelines. They'd discussed their hopes and dreams, but somehow putting it all together into a realistic, compatible, and *shared* career plan escaped them.

Not that there's anything particularly unusual about their lapse in planning. In fact, they were more communicative and motivated than many couples. They had just neglected to translate their goals into a joint plan, which is absolutely critical when you are career planning as a couple and have children to take into consideration as well. Understanding your individual goals and desires is one thing; determining how they fit together and affect your family is another entirely.

Where do you start when you're career planning as a couple, especially a role-reversed one? It's not as complicated as you might think. In fact, you've already begun the process by taking the career–family assessment and getting a sense of your ideal balance between work and family priorities.

Now, let's take it three steps further. Step 1 is for each of you to assess your individual career goals, Step 2 is for each of you to define your timetable to meet those goals, and Step 3—the crucial link for role-reversed parents—is for the two of you to lay those goals and timetables side by side and make sure they dovetail. That's the only way to ensure that the needs of the children are met while the short-term and long-term career objectives of both parents are addressed.

The Career Visualization Exercise:
A Hundred-Year Perspective

Before we get down to specific career goals, let's play a little travel-through-time game and visit your careers past, present, and future. This exercise will get you in touch with your deep-seated dreams and desires. If you currently feel stuck or know you aren't honoring your real passions, you need to do some soul-searching. Because even if you're not consciously aware of it, if you're off-track, those residual resentments can start to bubble up from inside and eat away not only at your confidence and ambition, but also at your relationship with your spouse. So, let's get ready to do some serious reflection here and see if you're really on the right career path or if you've settled for something less than what you truly want.

So here goes. Read this section through, then put the book aside while you try the exercise. Or if it's easier for you, have your spouse read it to you. Let your spouse read aloud in the most soothing voice he or she can muster up while you close your eyes, relax, and visualize.

First, find a spot where you won't be interrupted by phone, kids, or neighbors for a few minutes. Get yourself into a relaxed, meditative state, close your eyes, and let your mind wander over your career history. For those of you—dads or moms—who are now or have been full-time caregivers, think of that role as part of your career history.

Now picture your work history as a visual timeline. However it works best for you, seeing images on a movie screen or words on a roadside sign, start with your first job and visualize your way through your career. Your images don't need to be crystal clear. We're going for emotional truth here, not historical accuracy. Now, let your mind wander and watch those jobs lining up one after another. As you picture each one, from baby-sitting or working the fast-food window right up to now, ask yourself these questions:

1. How did each job make you feel?
2. Is there an element of the job—whether it's a person, a

place, or an activity—that you really enjoyed? That you hated?

3. Does part of you want to return to that job?
4. How would you feel if you went back? Would you do anything differently?
5. What did you learn on that particular job? As a worker? As a person?
6. What if you'd never had that job? Would your life have been different? Would you have been different?

Now, project yourself into the future—the distant future. Picture yourself at your hundredth birthday party. Your loved ones are gathered around; there's a big cake on the table with your name and a hundred candles on it. And you're listening intently as the adults around you are describing your life to the little ones who don't yet understand what it means to have the perspective of an entire century under your belt.

What do they say about you? How do they describe the cumulative accomplishments—both professional and personal—of a lifetime? What feels great when you hear it described? What's missing from this description of your work and life? Is there anything that you know you'd regret not being able to claim at that hundredth birthday celebration? Is there a career milestone that you'd always regret not having reached? Is there a personal accolade you'd want included? How does the balance between your work world and your family involvement sound?

Given the perspective of a century on your work and family life, what insights come up for you? For your partner? Are either of your surprised by your own or each other's reactions? Once you and your mate have talked over the results of this exercise, proceed to the next section.

Dreams and Deadlines: Steps 1 and 2

Now let's take that centenarian viewpoint and translate it into Step 1 of our career-planning process: goal setting. By now, you should have a better sense of how you and your spouse feel about balancing work and family, so let's see if we can turn that information into some specific career goals that address you, your partner, and your children. Don't worry if you think you won't remember every thought and image that came up during the career visualization exercise. It's all right there in your subconscious for you to call on whenever and however you need it.

First, make a list. Draw a vertical line down the center of a blank sheet of paper. On the left side write the heading "Goals"; on the right side, write the heading "Dates." Okay, here goes. Open up that mind again and just let it flow without thinking too much about what you're writing. It will all come.

On the "Goals" side of the page, make a list of all the career milestones you would like to accomplish in your lifetime. Don't make them complicated, just a word or two that will be a trigger and make sense to you. Write as many as you like. At this point, we are still casting a broad career net; later we will pull it in and separate out the big fish from the little ones, which we'll eventually throw back in the water. So start writing.

When you're finished, look back over your list. Amazing, isn't it, how many things you're interested in? When you're given permission to dream (not that you need it), it's really quite staggering how far your imagination can flow. Now comes the part that separates the dreamers from the doers. Look back over your goal list and, on the "Dates" side of the page, we're going to articulate a time frame specific to each goal as Step Two of the process.

For example, if you listed "Start my own baking business" or "Go back to work" in the "Goals" column, you'll write down the number of years it will take to accomplish that goal in the "Dates" column. If your target date for completing that goal is within one year, write a 1. If you want to accomplish it within twenty years, write 20. Just so you don't get too crazy with this, let's limit your choices to accomplishing your goals within the span of one year, three years, five years, ten years, twenty years, or a lifetime. Now go back and list your dates. You'll see your priorities start to emerge.

If you want to start your muffin business within one year, that tells you that that is a major priority. If you want to write your novel sometime in the next twenty years, maybe that is not such a pressing goal for you. However, if you want to write it within the next three years, it may be a real career objective, for which you need to start planning.

Your "Goals and Dates" charts might look something like this:

Bill's Goals	*Bill's Dates*
Write business plan	1 year
Network with promotions people	1 year
Attend promotions/consumer convention	1 year
Have own booth at convention	5 years
Launch promotions business	1 year
Finish master's degree	10 years
Build professional home office	1 year
Create company website	1 year

Angela's Goals	*Angela's Dates*
Continue to learn on job	ongoing
Build contacts in finance industry	ongoing
Speak on finance to local organizations	1 year
Get certification as financial planner	3 years
Launch home-based business as planner	5 years

Now, for those of you who said "Go back to work full-time," let's look at that for a minute. If you want to return to work within a year, you need to start some immediate planning. If you want to return to work within five years, you can still begin your planning phase now, but you'll have a much broader time frame. Are you beginning to see a pattern? Can you separate out the dreams from the goals? It's fine to dream, but some dreams are better left to the realm of fantasy. And then there are the goals that you're really committed to reaching. Now that you've got a sense of when you want to see these happen, you can begin to formulate a timeline that includes the interim steps that will allow each of you to reach your most important goals.

Step 3: Dovetailing Your Timelines

This is the step in which you and your spouse lay your timetables side by side and figure out how they might mesh harmoniously. Let's go back to Angela and Bill, the working wife and aspiring financial planner married to the at-home dad and aspiring marketer. When Bill and Angela realized their goals were out of sync and that they'd lost a sense of each other's commitments, they decided they needed to rebalance their priorities and get a better understanding of each other's career and family goals.

Here's what they did to get back on track. After they completed the balance assessment at the beginning of the chapter, it was clear to them that Angela was very happy to finally be out of school and working in her chosen field. When she understood that Bill was feeling frustrated and confined by his role as a stay-at-home dad, having cared for the kids full-time the entire three years Angela was in school and working full-time, she understood the importance *and* the urgency of his desire to launch his home-based business.

Bill, on the other hand, was completely willing to continue in his role as primary caregiver to allow Angela to get some career experience under her belt. He simply wanted the intellectual challenge and stimulation of starting the business that he'd fantasized about for years. He didn't expect it to skyrocket overnight and he didn't feel compelled to put in full-time hours at this point. Still, even though he was willing to start small and let it grow, Bill felt his new business was a now-or-never proposition.

Once they clearly understood their respective career objectives and how these would affect their overall family goals, Bill and

Angela sat down together to work out a joint timetable. They finally decided that Angela would continue in her new job for three to five years, growing and acquiring new skills with an eye toward eventually moving out on her own as a certified financial planner. Bill would immediately begin the research-and-development phase of his home-based marketing and promotion business. He would care for the kids and house, but he would work on his company while the children were in school. Bill decided to devote six months to the research phase, then another six months to building an initial clientele. Finally, Bill and Angela decided to reassess their goals and timeline every month and make course corrections as they went along.

Bill and Angela began to understand that they probably could attain many of their career goals—just not all at the same time. They also saw the importance of working together as a team, and that taking a backseat to each other's goals and dates at the appropriate time could bring them success both as individuals and as a couple. Most important, Bill and Angela realized that as a role-reversed couple, they could consciously arrange their lives to find the balance they desired between work and home.

As you compare your "Goals" and "Dates" charts with your partner, make sure you get to the heart of what's most important to each of you, and how best to divide and conquer in terms of your time and your resources. Also, be aware that these exercises are a jumping-off point and that your feelings, values, and goals will change, possibly often. Remember, you've committed your action plan to paper, not carved it in stone. You can—and should—sit down with your spouse regularly to reevaluate your goals and dates so you can keep the balance between home and career that's right for you.

One of the ways that balance can be achieved is through a "career switchback," as the at-home dad prepares to trade places with his spouse and return to the work world. Again, planning is the key to a successful transition.

Men at Work: The Career Switchback

One at-home dad describes his caregiver role as "the toughest job you can never quit." Sounds like a life sentence, doesn't it? And in some ways it is. Once you make the leap to parenthood, there's no turning back. But at-home parenting shouldn't be a punishment, even if it is an economic necessity.

Most SAHDs report that the most demoralizing part of the at-home dad experience is simply not knowing when or if they'll ever return to the workforce. With this common concern in mind, many forward-thinking role-reversed couples have mapped out their joint career paths with a built-in "career switchback" plan—a plan for when Dad might reenter the workforce. Sometimes just knowing there's a light at the end of the parenting tunnel is enough to keep you going until it's your turn to sit at a clean, Lego-free desk and take a phone call uninterrupted by boisterous, nap-deprived offspring.

For at-home dads who plan on rejoining the work world, it's never too early to develop a career reentry plan. You'll need to brush up on your skills, build the necessary contact base, and take whatever training courses you might need. Most of all, you'll need to get your confidence level back up to snuff by networking with other dads who've recently reentered the workforce, or by going on informational interviews in which no actual job is at stake but you can practice your interviewing skills.

Barry, the at-home dad we met in Chapter 2, is a part-time public relations writer and consultant, working for his local library system. The ability to work around his family's schedules made the job doable, but the intellectual stimulation made it fun. Now, Barry is considering another job in addition to the part-time one he already has. He's not sure he can commit to the hours, which he's made clear to his prospective employers, but he has decided to go on the interview as an exploratory opportunity. Barry feels it's important to keep his interviewing skills sharp and to keep building up his contacts, so that when he is ready to go back to work full-time, he'll already have a network.

Dads on the reentry plan may also want to consider easing back into a job by working part-time or even volunteering within their field. One extremely bright young at-home dad of a two-year-old, volunteered to work for Slowlane.com, the Internet SAHD resource guide. In a win-win scenario, this energetic SAHD gets to sharpen his online skills and build his contacts within the Internet and non-profit worlds, while at the same time supporting his SAHD/WM community.

Dads and Separation Anxiety

Dads going back to work will also need to prepare for the impact on their children. You'll need to have age-appropriate conversations to get your kids ready for your return to work. Whether both parents will be working or Mom and Dad will actually be switching places, the kids need to be prepped and eased into and through the transition. Remember Sam and Jackie from Chapter 6? Sam was the at-home dad who decided to go back to work once his daughters were ten and twelve. It was only when the kids protested in panic that he rethought his decision.

But dads, that's not always the case. In fact, the kids may adjust to the change much more quickly than you do. Many dads who return to the workforce report that they experience an enormous sense of loss. Miles was a longtime at-home dad who decided that once his three boys all hit high school, it was time to get a job. Overcoming his own fears about outdated skills, a spotty résumé, and the possibility he might absentmindedly cut a co-worker's steak into little pieces one day at lunch, Miles took the plunge. The boys all adjusted quite well. It was Miles who suffered a very real depression about not being there when his guys got home from school, not being the first one to hear the news of the day, and, to his surprise, not being the one who actually felt a sense of pride at having dinner on the table every night at 6:30. But in talking to other former SAHDs, Miles discovered they had all gone through some form of withdrawal from their old life and, they assured him, he, too, would adjust with time.

The Work-at-Home Dad

Some men, like web developer Jay and 25 million Americans (about half of whom are part-timers), may prefer to work at home. Whether the demands of your home-based business require you to get outside help to care for the kids or you can juggle (join the juggling working moms!) caring for kids and working at home, you and your wife will need to go through the career planning exercise presented earlier in the chapter. Together, sit down and review your short and long-term goals, priorities, and timelines. See if you agree on how many hours each of you will be working, whether there will be travel involved, and who will be available for the many activities and needs of your children.

Another possibility for the work-at-home dad (or mom) is telecommuting—working at home, but for an employer, not in your own business. With advanced technologies, more workers than ever before now telecommute.

Working-Mom Guilt and the Juggling Act

If you're one of the 25 million working moms out there, watch out, because sooner or later you're bound to fall right into the guilt trap. It seems to be unavoidable, at least occasionally. But understanding what this guilt is all about can help you climb out of the trap and get back on solid ground.

Now that women are widely accepted into almost all areas of the workplace, they are slowly being let in on a little secret that working dads have been privy to all along. Work can actually be fun. That's right, you heard it here. Men have known all along that the right job—not just any job, but the right job—can be extremely rewarding, and not just monetarily.

In fact, the workplace with all its challenges, intellectual stimulation, and office friendships, can be very seductive. Factor in the salary—especially now that almost 25 percent of working wives earn more than their husbands—and career women can get downright giddy.

But there is a price to pay. Most working women cite guilt as the number one drawback of their careers. And what do they feel guilty about? The question is, what do they *not* feel guilty about? Not surprisingly, working moms who hold down jobs purely for economic reasons report an overwhelming sense of guilt at being away from their children, even when an at-home dad takes care of the kids full-time. But even moms who choose to go to work and feel no qualms about having Dad at home raising the kids can feel enormous guilt. Why? Because these moms don't feel entitled to enjoy their work as much as they do. They're still plagued by society's age-old belief that women should be home with their children.

Second only to guilt in its impact on working moms is the intensity and pervasiveness of the juggling act, otherwise known as obligation overload. Here's a question for you: Do you know anyone who's complained recently about life being too sedate? It seems that the more technological advances are available to us—which, in theory at least, should simplify our lives—the more intense and hectic our lives become. We can literally be on call at work, via some device or other, twenty-four hours a day. With our twenty-first-century computers, cell phones, fax machines, and e-mail, we seem to be chained to our work even more completely than toilers in a nineteenth-century sweatshop.

Here's a simple measure of the accelerated pace of our working-mom lives. Ask someone how they are and see if they answer "crazed" or "swamped" with pride or with dismay. The scary thing is, we are slowly convincing ourselves that overcomplicating our multitasked lives is a good thing. So how can working moms combat the two-headed dragon of guilt and overload? Try these suggestions on for size:

- Talk frankly with your spouse about work/family priorities, and reevaluate your respective career plans periodically. This will make you feel less guilty and therefore less stressed. Don't forget to use and reuse the assessment quiz, visualization exercise, "Goals and Dates" list, and timeline detailed in this chapter.

- Put limits on your availability to your work. For example, decide that you won't answer work-related phone calls (cell or otherwise), faxes, or e-mails after seven p.m. during the week, or anytime during the weekend. Family-friendly boundaries will help you relieve stress and maintain a better balance in your life. If your boss or workplace can't abide by such standards, maybe it's time to consider a different job.

- Don't let friends, relatives, or co-workers sway you into feeling guilty about how you and your spouse are going about providing for and attending to your family. Gather strength from your spouse, other allies, and the SAHD/WM community.

- Schedule enough time for physical exercise, getting together with friends, and just relaxing on your own. Try reading a book or magazine that isn't work-related, every now and then. Make an appointment to do these things, and keep the date as conscientiously as you would a business engagement.

Career planning can be a challenge, but it can also be an exciting joint opportunity for you and your spouse to build the life you want for yourselves and your children. The key is that you do it in concert with each other. You've got a whole family depending on your teamwork. And just think what an example you'll set for your children—to forge the kinds of careers they want free from limiting stereotypes, to appropriately balance work and family commitments, and to create rewarding lives of passion and power.

Quick Review

Now that you've rewritten your work-family roles, keep in mind that they are not written in stone. They are meant to be flexible and fluid. But, once again, planning is the name of the game.

Assess your career and family goals.

Mom and Dad should each take the career-family assessment quizzes in this chapter to gain clarity on values and goals. Now share your results and use those responses to start, or deepen, a dialogue with your spouse about what each of you really wants. You may decide to revisit the quizzes periodically to reassess your work-family balance on an ongoing basis.

By definition, career planning for couples is a shared exercise.

Don't forget that role-reversed couples need to take each other and the children into consideration in their career planning. But it's not as difficult as you may think. Follow the three steps indicated in this chapter, then share the results, to create a balanced work-family plan.

- Step One: Assess your individual career goals.
- Step Two: Define your timetable to meet those goals.
- Step Three: Both of you lay your goals and timetables side by side to make sure they are compatible.

There are special considerations for SAHDs reentering the workforce.

Dads need to develop a career reentry plan, including brushing up on their skills and building a contact base so that when they're ready to return, they've got the network and the knowledge to get the job. Dads should also be prepared to deal with the separation anxiety that their kids—and they themselves—may experience once they leave their at-home jobs behind.

Working at home can be an interim compromise or a long-term career solution.

For many dads around the country, working at home can be the ideal career solution, either short or long-term. It can allow dad the opportunity to keep his skills strong, contribute financially to the family, and still be a full-time caregiver. Telecommuting, i.e. working at home for an employer other than yourself, is another great option for SAHDS who want to be WAHDS (work-at-home dads).

Guilt and stress may go with the territory, working moms, but there are plenty of things you can do to counteract them.

Sooner or later, most working moms succumb to either guilt or obligation overload, or both. But there are some ways to combat the two-headed dragon.

- Spell out your work-family priorities and obligations to your spouse. If they're out in the open (and on the calendar) then you can plan for them in advance, and alleviate a lot of stress in the process.
- Establish some appropriate work-related boundaries, like no nonemergency phone calls on the weekends. Create your own family-friendly workplace by articulating your needs to your boss and colleagues and if they're not receptive, maybe it's time to rethink your place of employment.
- Don't fall into the Guilt Trap. Enlist support from people who appreciate your lifestyle.
- Schedule physical exercise, dates with friends, just plain downtime, like you would a business appointment—and stick to it.

Chapter 8

Sexual Sparks in the SAHD/WM Marriage

I ronic, isn't it? You had sex to get the kids, and now that you've got the kids, you hardly ever have time for sex anymore. Sound familiar? Well, you're not alone. Just ask around. Plenty of parents have precisely the same complaint.

Meet Scott and Maria, both in their mid-thirties, married for eight years with two kids. Conscientious about making time for themselves as a couple, they have the perfect evening planned. It's the kind of night both of them have treasured ever since they fell in love. Nothing fancy, no big occasion. Just the chance to spend a quiet evening at home together. To linger over a good meal, drink a nice glass of wine, and talk about the events of the day and their hopes for the future.

Their plans for tonight went something like this: First, Scott would call Maria at the office around four, reminding her of their date and asking her to pick up a bottle of the Merlot they both like on her way home from work. No problem, she assured him. She'd duck out of her five o'clock meeting by six sharp and be home, ready for a night of relaxed romance, by seven.

Scott would have his famous marinara sauce simmering as he

fed the kids, then bathed them and got them ready for bed. By the time Maria walked in the front door, their little darlings—two-year-old Madeleine and ten-month-old André—would be ready to be kissed, tucked in, and put down for the night. Maria and Scott would have the entire evening to unwind, enjoy a candlelit dinner, then move on to a night of uninterrupted passion.

Not.

Well, so much for the fantasy version of the life of a working mom, a stay-at-home dad, and two small, very demanding children. Here's what really happened on Scott and Maria's date night.

First, Scott called Maria to remind her that he was attempting to prepare a civilized meal for the two of them. It had been weeks since either of them had eaten a dinner that wasn't Chinese take-out or something nuked in the microwave, and he was afraid that they might forget how to use utensils if they didn't sit at the table and eat like normal adults for a change. Maria, who had completely forgotten about their date, panicked because she had a late meeting that she knew she couldn't miss. Then, typically, she felt a huge pang of guilt for putting her job before her husband, even though she was the sole breadwinner and her work was undeniably critical to the family's well-being.

So, setting yet another spinning plate in motion, Maria told Scott not to worry, she'd be home right on time. When he asked her to stop and pick up a bottle of wine, she was ready to protest: how would she ever find the extra ten minutes needed to dash into the store to make the purchase, and still get home remotely on time? But squelching her familiar stress reaction, she added one more platter to the spin cycle and told her husband, No problem.

Scott, meanwhile, was struggling to make his scratch marinara sauce and simultaneously watch two active youngsters. But when Madeleine smacked André in a fit of jealous rage, Scott knew he didn't dare leave the two of them unattended for even a moment. He gave up on his marinara and opened a jar of spaghetti sauce, hoping he could disguise it with some added spices. By the time Maria got home, he had just finished scraping André's strained apricots off the wall and ditched the idea of a bath in favor of mopping up both kids with a kitchen towel.

By then, it was nearly eight. Maria's meeting had run late and she'd just realized that she'd forgotten to pick up the wine, as she stowed her briefcase and cell phone for the night, praying no one from the office would call her at home. Madeleine and André, even though they were happy to see Mom, started their ritual nightly meltdown to let off the cumulative exhaustion of the day. As Maria tried futilely to comfort them, Scott reluctantly turned off the stove and helped his wife wrestle the screaming children into their pajamas.

Not exactly your idea of foreplay? It certainly wasn't Scott and Maria's. But it is a realistic picture of family life today and how the constant juggling, nonstop energy-draining activity and relentless demands on our time affect the sexual relationship of overburdened parents. The only thing that might make it even more trying would be if both Mom and Dad worked outside the home. Then both, instead of just one of them, would come rushing in at seven or eight, exhausted from the day's labors and anxious to catch up with their caregiver about their child's day—the day both parents had missed and would never recapture.

But sex doesn't have to take a backseat to work and parenting. At least, not all the time. There really is romantic hope for sex-deprived parents, even those of you with infants, even newborn multiples—*yikes!*—at home. All it takes is a little discipline, advance planning, and a few good substitute, part-time caregivers! But we're getting ahead of ourselves. First, let's take a look at the part role-reversal plays in the sexual dynamic of a marriage. Because, acknowledged or not, it definitely plays a part.

Interestingly, many SAHDs report that their working wives are so thrilled with their parenting arrangement—particularly those women who really prefer to be on the job, like Elizabeth, the high-powered attorney we met in Chapter 2—that they are more sexually responsive to their husbands than if both adults were working. Many SAHDs say they "get more action" not only than traditional working dads but often than their single friends as well.

But role reversal doesn't always enhance a couple's sexual relationship. And if SAHD/WM couples aren't willing to explore their own feelings about their role reversal, especially fears and prejudices surrounding masculinity and femininity, their role reversal can create distance, or even animosity, in the marriage.

Let's take a closer look at Scott and Maria. Plenty of parents, no matter what their lifestyle configuration, can relate to their nightly three-ring circus. But what was actually going on beneath the surface was that Scott and Maria were using the demands of the day as a distraction from their real intimacy issues. Neither wanted to acknowledge that their feelings of sexual attraction were beginning to fade—and that their role reversal played a part. Fortunately, Scott recognized the problem before it went too far and talked it over with Maria. With some professional help, they realized that, rather than face the difficult issues regarding their role-reversed marriage, they had chosen to ignore their feelings. Once these issues were out on the table, Maria and Scott began to rebuild their intimacy and create an even stronger partnership.

And Scott and Maria's experience is far from an isolated case. As the euphoric honeymoon phase of marriage naturally begins to fade, keeping the sexual spark alive is difficult for any couple. But for SAHD/WM couples, emotions like guilt, powerlessness, and anger can make it even more difficult.

Because It's Not Just About Sex

It's also about our socialization and conditioning with respect to traditional concepts of masculinity and femininity, with a healthy dose of competition and power struggling thrown in for good measure. In plain English, most of us weren't brought up to believe that men could be successful caregivers and women could support not just themselves—we've accepted that—but their entire families.

No wonder you're exhausted and overwhelmed. You're trying to keep a marriage on track and a career on course, and at the same time, you're raising children (or at least contemplating it). That's enough right there to make you scream in surrender. And now you've got this added pressure as a role-reversed couple? Maybe, if you're well into your gender swap, you think you've navigated all the marital whitewater already. Or, if you're just now in the thinking-about-it stage, maybe you're confident that you can handle all those issues without breaking a sweat. Just don't ignore them altogether, even if they're a bit uncomfortable to discuss with your mate.

If you've already embarked on your role-reversed parenting adventure, you're probably used to comments about how "lucky" the two of you are—as if this unique arrangement fell out of the sky and landed in your laps. By now, you've also undoubtedly encountered all those pesky issues about chores and parenting styles. But have you really thought about how your role reversal has affected the sexual dynamic of your relationship?

Thinking—and talking—through some of these issues before they become problems can really help. And just as the basic start-up plan we discussed in Chapter 3 can help you work out your parenting roles, the questions below can help focus your thinking about your sexuality. So take a moment to answer the questions below, separately or with your mate, and then openly discuss the issues they bring up.

Has Your Role-Reversed Lifestyle Affected Your Sex Life?

- Would you rather sleep than have sex?
- Does sex feel more like a chore than a pleasure?
- For wives: Was your husband sexier when he got up in the morning and went to the office/factory/showroom/whatever than he does now that he gets up to take care of the kids?
- For husbands: Do you ever worry that your wife will find the men at work more attractive than you, simply because they are working full-time outside the home?
- For wives: Have you ever felt compelled to defend your husband's masculinity in light of his status as an at-home dad?

- For husbands: Do you feel your that full-time parenting has made you less sexually aggressive—e.g. do you initiate sex less often, are you less adventurous or confident?
- For wives: Do you feel that being the family breadwinner also puts you in charge as the sexual aggressor?
- Do you have trouble turning off your role as either caregiver or breadwinner in the bedroom?
- Does either of you think the wife would be/feel more feminine if she were a full-time mom?
- Does either of you think the husband would be/feel more masculine if he were the breadwinner?
- Is your sex life really satisfying?
- What do you think you could do to make it better?

Take some time to really think about these questions and then discuss your responses with each other. Talk about the ways in which trading places in the workaday world complicates your sex life, in both practical and emotional ways. Once you realize that your less-than-sizzling sex life is not *just* about the sex, or your lack of time and energy, but all this other stuff heaped on top of it, then you can begin to sort out your conflicted feelings and open up an honest dialogue with your mate.

And when you begin to look at your sexual relationship through the gender-role filter, it's easy to see why the breadwinning wife who has spent the day locked in corporate battle, buried in office tedium, or somewhere in between the two, has difficulty turning on her feminine, sexual side the minute she walks in the door and drops her briefcase. But, at least the working wife is living in the outside world, interacting with people who view her as a woman, not just a mom or a breadwinner. Even if she is a construction crew supervisor, she is out in the world experiencing her power as a working woman, contributing to her family and society. Or maybe it goes even further than that. She may be acknowledged for her attractiveness, her intelligence, her personality, maybe even her flirtatiousness. She may feel vital because she stays on top of trends, and dresses the part that her job requires. She feels important, alive, part of the greater community. And, as an added bonus, she probably gets to eat at restaurants with no kids' meals.

Now think how it might be debilitating for a stay-at-home dad. All day long, he's been turning gender stereotypes on their ears. He's wearing an apron, changing diapers, and dropping off kids at preschool. Trying to convince the neighbors, the teachers, and the checker at the market that he's not some pedophile or deadbeat but a loving and dedicated dad who has made a conscious choice to father his children, even if it means he's the only man in the neighborhood who takes his daughter to Brownies. Worse, all the while his wife is on the job talking to guys who wear ties, don't need an allowance, and drive sports cars instead of mini-vans. Doesn't exactly make a guy feel like a hunk of burning love, does it?

Reigniting the Sparks

Now that you have some understanding of what you've been up against, what are you supposed to do about it? Like many successful SAHD/WM couples, you need to get creative. Here are some of their ideas for re-igniting the sexual sparks in your relationship.

Opposites Attract

Kevin and Faith have been married for sixteen years and have a fourteen-year-old son. They found they liked to spice things up by playing out their sexual fantasies, particularly those that put a spin on the role reversal they were living. Faith, a high-powered sales rep, discovered that she enjoyed being sexually dominated by her at-home husband and that their lovemaking was heightened by role-playing fantasies that were counter to their daily experience. Kevin, on the other hand, had long since come to grips with being the sensitive caregiver, but also enjoyed the sense of power and control that his dominating role in the bedroom afforded him. The introduction of sex toys and pornographic videos further enhanced their sex play and kept their relationship fresh, particularly after so many years together.

The Role-Reversal Reversal

Another technique that some couples have found particularly effective is consciously dropping their role reversal when the working wife comes home from the office. David, an at-home dad of three-year-old twin boys, found that when his wife Robyn, a high-school principal, would purposely abandon her work mode upon coming home and jump into a more traditional female role—cooking dinner, putting the kids to bed—it put both of them in a much sexier mood. On the other hand, when David continued his at-home role throughout the evening and Robyn hung on to her workday, it put a damper on their sexual feelings for each other. Thanks to an astute marriage counselor and some courageous exploration, they realized what worked for them sexually and began to consciously switch roles at the end of each day. Eventually the "role-reversal reversal," as they called it, came naturally, and they spontaneously fell into more traditional roles at the end of the day, giving them both a break from their routines and an enhanced appreciation of one another as sexual beings.

If you're thinking it's a drag to have to work at creating sexual feelings for each other, wake up and smell the baby formula. This is marriage, and if you're in it for the long haul, you have to traverse some road bumps along the way. It doesn't come by magic, wishing, or dreaming. You create the reality, and if it ain't working, you better figure out how to fix it. The good news is, once you decide to address your concerns head-on instead of pretending they don't exist, you can make some really positive changes that can fuel your marriage and provide the heat for years to come.

Planned Spontaneity

Adelle and Byron, a long-time SAHD/WM couple, had three daughters, ages sixteen, twelve, and nine. Married for eighteen years, they were best friends and life partners. Divorce statistics notwithstanding, their passionate relationship had deepened into a bond that both Byron and Adelle were sure would sustain a lifetime. The problem was, being best friends and life partners didn't feel all that sexy. So they decided to do something about it. This creative couple initiated a regular, ongoing sexual strategy they called planned spontaneity. Whenever they felt a little icy in the romance department, they planned a "spontaneous" adventure to turn up the heat in their marriage. Either one of them could initiate the adventure—anything from an evening at home or a night on the town to a mini vacation. The important thing was that the focus be on the two of them, as a loving and sexual couple. As a precaution, Byron and Adelle also made a rule that they would have at least one spontaneous episode a month—for the rest of their lives. Lifetime planning may seem like the antithesis to spontaneity, but it certainly kept the spark alive for this enduring couple.

Face it. Ever since you became parents, spontaneity has gotten to be pretty much a thing of the past. But you knew that when you decided to have kids, didn't you? You were willing to forgo those lazy weekend mornings in bed with your second cup of coffee and the Sunday *Times*. You fully understood that the two of you wouldn't be jumping into the car and heading off on a wild last-minute adventure every time you felt like it. But did you really think your sex life would take such a nosedive? Whatever you envisioned when you planned to have a family, giving up on the romantic part of your relationship was definitely not part of the deal. Nor does it have to be.

But you do need a healthy dose of realism about how to rebuild, if not actual spontaneity, then something that approximates it. Unlike real spontaneity, planned spontaneity requires that you work out the details ahead of time—sort of like the advance team for the president—but once you do, you'll give your relationship a framework so you can relax and have some fun together. And that's when you can rekindle those romantic fires and immerse yourselves in each other again. But it means getting all your daily demands—house, kids, and job—out of the way so you can recon-nect with your mate.

That's where Scott and Maria got off-track. Part of their sexual self-sabotage was allowing the distractions and demands of work and childcare to interfere with real, intimate couple time. Once they began to confront those issues, they increased their chances of success dramatically by adding a baby-sitter to their date night and getting out of the house for dinner once or twice a month. By the time they came home, the kids were in bed and they were free to continue their night of romance.

Once you've got this concept of planned spontaneity under your belt and it becomes second nature, you'll see how it can mag-ically transform the context of your sexual partnership. Dis-cussing, arranging, and then addressing the details and logistics of being together can clear the path for dramatic changes that can deeply affect your marriage and your level of sexual satisfaction. And it's not just sex that will be affected. As you begin to master the art of planned spontaneity, you'll find that understanding each other's needs and working as a team to carve out "together time" turns even the everyday moments in your life into intimate times.

Isn't It Romantic?

Suppose you and your spouse have sorted out all the issues that might be affecting your sexuality—including those related to who works inside and outside your home, and how each of you per-ceives masculinity and femininity. You've also discussed how your role reversal manifests in your sexuality, and how to create more spontaneity in your sex life. Whew! If you didn't need some time off for romance before, you certainly do after all that work. Exactly how do you find, make, or steal that precious couple time?

Here are a few tricks from the pros—that is, the role-swapped parents who have been there and done that. They've suffered through the sexual droughts and survived to see another rainfall, thanks to their creativity, flexibility, and open communication. So what do they recommend? Here goes.

Never Miss Date Night

You're feeling pressured already, just by the title? You say you have work, chores, PTA meetings, religious gatherings, family functions? How the heck are you supposed to work a date night into all that? No one said date night had to be every night, or even once a week, but putting aside a little special time once a month for your life partner certainly doesn't seem like too much to ask. Who knows, it might be so much fun you'll find a way to make it work more often.

Barring parents with newborns, who are pretty much slaves to their infants for those first few months anyway, the following plan should work for just about anyone. It's really very simple.

Put your date night on the calendar. And if you don't have a family calendar posted in the kitchen or some other central, high-traffic area, what are you waiting for? You can put it in pencil if you like—remember, flexibility is the key here—but if you don't put it down in writing, it will mysteriously disappear, just like those socks that go in the dryer but never come out.

Decide how much time you want away from home and kids. You don't have to figure out what you're doing or where you're going—yet. Just establish the time block, but make it substantial enough for the two of you to unwind, stop talking about the kids, house, and bills, and to get into the couple-having-fun-together mode. Three hours is probably the minimum. But, once again, flexibility is key; if you can only manage a couple of hours, it's a lot better than skipping your date altogether.

Work out the logistics. First, you need to work out your child-care logistics, but don't forget about the adult logistics, too. Get your kidcare worked out—a sitter, the next-door neighbor (whom you'll repay in kind), or Grandma and Grandpa. Get it booked on their calendar as well, so they know it's not just some little casual thing. It's a big deal to get out, so make it sound like one, even if you have to embellish a bit. Next, figure out the grown-up logistics. Can Mom get away from the office on time if this is a weekday date? Does Dad have Boy Scouts, homework, or other family-related activity that he needs to reschedule or reprioritize? Work it out early because, as anyone with kids already knows, last-minute stuff *always* comes up.

Just say, "Date." Okay, you've set the date, you've conquered all the logistical problems, and you're good to go. Now what? Whatever you want. You can plan a romantic dinner, go to the movies, stroll on the beach. Whatever gets your romantic juices flowing and reunites you as a couple. Try not to pressure yourselves to have a great time, great sex, or anything else extraordinary. Overblown expectations are sure to stop your own natural flow of energy. Just go with it and have some fun. You deserve it. If you feel more comfortable taking a beeper or cell phone along, do it. Just don't take calls unless they're of the 911 variety. And don't forget to agree on a statute of limitations with regard to talking about kids and home, so you don't spend your entire evening deciding whether to get the dishwasher repaired or buy a new one. That would definitely not be a good use of your "romantic" time. It takes some practice to get out of parental mode and back into what brought you together in the first place. But practicing can be fun!

Plan the next date immediately. Don't think, just because you got your act together once and went out on an actual date, that you're through. Now it's time to plan another while the spirit is still moving you. So put a date on the calendar again. You might even want to think about making dates weekly instead of monthly, or monthly instead of semiannually if that's where you're currently stuck.

Quarterly Romantic Retreat

Now that you've mastered the art of the night out, you're ready for the big time. A weekend away with no kids, no pets, no grandparents. If you've gone into shock, breathe deeply, then pick yourself up off the floor and contemplate the luxury of an entire weekend alone with your spouse. No alarm clocks, human or otherwise. No briefcase, no sandboxes, no Little League. Whatever you want to do, including nothing, the weekend is yours.

The planning process for pulling off the romantic retreat is similar to the night out. Just expand the process to include childcare for the entire weekend and cover your own logistics as well. If you're panicking at the prospect of leaving your kids for a whole weekend, start small. Try booking a hotel room or going camping close by for one night only. You can work your way up to an entire weekend as your kids get older. The beauty is, they adjust to the change right along with you and come to expect Mommy and Daddy's dates as a matter of course. A little healthy role modeling on your part. Aren't you the clever ones?

But hold on, you're saying, this just wouldn't work for you. Your life is too complicated.

Interesting. Somehow you manage to come up with logistical solutions to the complex tangle of work/kids/household/community obligations every day. And you're such an expert at it that you could qualify for the White House advance team. Yet when it comes to planning some alone time for you and your spouse, you're stumped. If this is the case, you'd better take a look at why you're resisting the scheduling of this romantic time for you and your mate—before your romance slips away entirely, as it almost did for Scott and Maria.

And don't think that date night or the romantic retreat have to be costly, either. One young couple, Jonelle and Alan, took a novel approach to keeping their romantic life flying high. Despite limited funds and the demands of a three-year-old, they managed to create their own version of a weekly date night. Every Wednesday, after they put their son, Jared, to bed, they would have a "bedroom picnic." With candles, romantic CDs, a bottle of wine, and whatever take-out they pulled together, dinner on a blanket on the floor became their own private getaway.

This romantic picnic was also their special brand of foreplay for an evening of lovemaking they both looked forward to all week. Not that they waited for that night; they had a healthy ongoing sexual relationship. But picnic night also came to include a sexual picnic: Jonelle and Alan would explore fantasies, role-playing, sex toys, videos, whatever their lusty souls decided to explore. That night became so important to them, that when Jonelle got her first big promotion and their money situation eased up a bit, they celebrated by booking a weekend away and had a forty-eight-hour picnic, never leaving their hotel room once. Now, that's a romantic retreat we could all use on a quarterly basis!

A Parent's Right to Privacy

Love and sex form the foundation of your marriage. But while it's great to show your kids the love, respect, and caring that you and your mate have for each other, and while it's fine for them to see that you and your spouse enjoy a healthy lust for each other, sex is a private matter.

Setting aside the issue of actually telling your kid about sex—let's talk about what you think is appropriate for your child to see or know about your romantic relationship with your spouse. Obviously, this isn't an issue for infants or very small children, but sooner than you think, certainly by toddler time, kids begin to pick up messages about how their parents relate to one another, and often those messages are powerful enough to last a lifetime. So let's make sure you are sending the messages you want your kids to internalize.

First, you need to determine your basic ground rules for privacy. Teach your kids from the time they are small that your bedroom is a sanctuary and that, while they are warmly welcomed into it at times, there are other times when it is off-limits. Some parents believe in locking their bedroom door. Others feel that doing so is an affront to family members and, instead, teach their youngsters that they must knock before entering the adults' private space. Just remember, this is a golden opportunity for you to model precisely the behavior you want from your children, so make sure you get in the habit of knocking before you enter their bedrooms, too.

Kerry and Daniel wished they had thought about privacy issues *before* their twelve-year-old daughter, Lyssa, walked in on them in the middle of lovemaking one summer night. It was after midnight, and they assumed she had long since fallen asleep, so they never gave a thought to shutting their bedroom door, especially since Lyssa was a sound sleeper and her room was at the other end of the house. But when an upset stomach woke her up, she went looking for comfort and Tums and instead found Kerry astride her husband in an obvious moment of intense passion.

Busted, Kerry could only roll over and pull the bedcovers up around herself. Daniel tried mightily to pretend everything was all healthy and normal, but in truth felt as if he had just plopped his impressionable adolescent daughter down in front of a porno flick.

Kerry put on her bathrobe and tended to her daughter's stomach, then sat her down and discussed, openly and honestly, what she had just seen. It wasn't the first conversation they'd had about sex. Daniel and Kerry were very straightforward about the subject and wanted to give their daughter as much truthful information as they felt was appropriate. They had just never anticipated telling Lyssa about sex in relation to their own lives. Once Lyssa got over the initial shock and subsequent gross-out factor—"You and Dad do *what*?"—Kerry and Daniel's resilient preteen recovered from both stomachaches.

Kerry and Daniel's story is, of course, a fairly extreme example of the need to establish boundaries with your children. You should also think about all the everyday stuff. For example, are you comfortable with your children seeing you passionately kiss your spouse? Not just a good-bye peck, but a serious liplock? You may feel a little silly discussing this with your mate, but believe it or not, it matters. And it's much easier to decide these questions when the kids are little. Do you want to "go public" or keep such sensual displays private? And if you're okay with going public, how far do you go? To display or not to display, that is the question. Setting comfortable boundaries will ensure that your kids are protected from what they're not meant to see, and that you and your mate have the privacy you're entitled to.

Sexual Connection

As parents, sometimes we have to remind ourselves that we are also sexual beings. It's very easy to get caught up in letting everything and everybody else come first. But despite the daily stresses of childcare, finances, career, extended family, friends, and chores, we should never neglect the sexual connection to our mate. The relentless minutiae of life don't ease up when we're caring for home and family, so we have to make a conscious decision to get off the treadmill once in a while and reconnect with our partner.

And if your other half is half of a SAHD/WM couple, really look at your role reversal and see how it affects your sexual partnership. If you need help, seek out a professional counselor, a religious practitioner, or talk to other at-home dad/working mom couples. Just being aware of the challenges that a role-reversal relationship can add to your sexuality as individuals and as a couple is half the battle.

Most of all, don't lose sight of the fact that plenty of parents before you have managed to keep the marital flames burning. So remember how you got those kids in the first place and keep fanning those sexual sparks!

Quick Review

Every parent knows that having kids can put a strain on the sex life. It just goes with the territory, like late-night feedings and runny noses. But being a role-reversed couple can add another layer of sexual challenge. This chapter provides some creative solutions straight from the SAHD/WMs themselves.

Recognize that, as in other areas of your rule-rewritten lives, trading traditional roles can have an effect on your sexuality.

Take the sex quiz to see where you and your mate really stand with regard to your sexuality. Once you acknowledge that you may be facing some pressures that more traditional couples just don't have to deal with, you can begin to discuss your feelings about your sex life and make some positive changes. And if your sex life is in good shape already, just think how great it will be after you try these tips for keeping the home fires burning.

Keep fanning those sexual sparks.

- Try "role-reversal reversal," that is, consciously trade roles back so that *he* takes on the more traditionally dominant role and *she* takes on the more feminine, submissive role. Granted, these may feel like the old stereotypical roles, but if they're atypical for you, that can be just enough to make them exciting.
- Give "planned spontaneity" a go. Don't expect romance to happen magically, plan for it.
- Get a date on the calendar for your "never miss date night."
- Work your way up to the "quarterly romantic retreat" and try a weekend away from home and kids. It can do wonders for your romance.

It's never too early to teach your kids about privacy.

In addition to providing some healthy role-modeling, taking steps to ensure your privacy can give you the freedom to explore your sexuality without worrying that a kid is going to show up in the bedroom unannounced. Parents have rights too, you know.

Chapter 9

Summing It All Up

The ABCs of Successful Role Reversal

S AHD/WM couples are a very generous lot, eager to share their parenting triumphs and tribulations. This chapter will sum up all the advice you've read throughout this book by looking more closely at some trend-setting couples and how they've overcome specific challenges. We'll also focus on the three essential qualities of role-reversed parenting. That is, the ABCs of the SAHD/WM lifestyle: Appreciation, Balance, and Communication.

"Breaking Through the Linoleum Floor"

They don't call Bill Laut the Iron Man of Stay-at-Home Dads for nothing. Bill, and his wife, Sheila, are the parents of triplets. And not just triplets. Toddler triplets, as in, count 'em, three three-year-olds. You want to talk role reversal challenges, Bill and Sheila have seen it all. They even wrote a book, *Raising Multiple Birth Children: A Parents' Survival Guide*, to help out other parents of multiples who were faced with what they call the DINK-to-

SINK syndrome—double income/no kids to single income/numerous kids.

Sheila is a sales management executive for a large corporation. It's a demanding job and requires extensive travel. Bill, who holds an MBA in finance, ran his own contracting business before he became an around-the-clock dad. They faced all the typical role-reversed family challenges, plus a few atypical ones brought on strictly by their multiple status, when they decided they needed a full-time parent at home. As with many of the other couples we've met so far, finances played a big part in Bill and Sheila's decision. Daycare times three was simply not an economic option for the Lauts, even if they had been predisposed to outsourcing the care and feeding of their trio. Because Sheila's job offered excellent benefits, which they sorely needed for their large instant family, they decided that Bill would shut down his contracting business and stay home with the kids. The Lauts say it was a surprisingly easy decision and one they haven't regretted for a moment.

But it hasn't always been an easy ride. In fact, toddler-ready vehicle notwithstanding, it's never been an easy ride. When other parents of newborns were sleep-deprived, Bill and Sheila were practically zombies. And when those new parents were shelling out their hard-earned dollars for packs of Huggies, the Lauts were shelling out times three. To make matters more complicated, Sheila was often traveling, sometimes out of the country for extended periods of time, and Bill was on his own with the three babies. He welcomed help from his friends and family and advises other parents, and not just those of multiples, to do the same. "Most people don't offer unless they really want to help," Bill suggests, "and they're actually flattered when you take them up on their generosity." Just make sure that you tell your volunteers exactly what help you need, whether it's watching the kids so Mom or Dad can nap, fixing a casserole, or doing the laundry. That way, you get done what you need done and they don't have to flounder, wondering if they're really helping out or just in the way.

Bill says that while Sheila is more career-driven and successful, he is by far the more patient and flexible of the two, a prerequisite for at-home status that other dads mention resoundingly and often. Like other couples, Bill and Sheila got some negative reactions from others, most notably a subtle lack of respect for Bill's decision to put his career on hold. A decision, he is quick to point out, that is not etched in stone but always open to future negotiation with his wife.

A strong guy, both physically and emotionally, Bill believes that being an at-home dad, especially of triplets, has made him even stronger. He cautions new stay-at-home dads and their wives to make their own decisions, to do what they feel is right for their families, not what society dictates. When people ask him how it feels "not to work," he no longer feels compelled to suggest they switch places with him for an hour or so and find out just how challenging "not working" can be. Instead, he just lets the remark roll off. As Bill sees it, "women have been breaking through the glass ceiling for a while; now it's time for men to break through the linoleum floor." And if anyone can do it, this Iron Man is just the guy.

A Is for Attitude

As Bill and Sheila quickly discovered, role reversal is all about attitude. It's about maintaining perspective and a sense of humor. When the triplets are getting to be too much, Bill says he has to step back in order to keep his cool. He recommends that at-home parents who feel like they're losing it step away—go anywhere they can get a moment's peace. In Bill and Sheila's case, that was usually the laundry room, and "meet me in the laundry room" quickly became a running joke as well as a parental lifesaver for this children-challenged couple. Bill firmly believes that you have to be a happy person if you're going to raise a happy person, or in his case, three happy people. And to do that, you need to recognize when you need an attitude adjustment.

Appreciation

Attitude is also about appreciation. Pete, a part-time graphics designer and full-time SAHD, is a warm and outgoing father raising a little girl with his wife, Jessica, an executive for a global telecommunications company. Pete, who recently followed his wife halfway around the world for her career, recalls a time early in their marriage when he felt unappreciated by her. Although personal and painful, his feeling is echoed by many other at-home dads who have felt underappreciated, or even disrespected, by their working wives, as less than equal in the partnership.

What Pete came to believe about role reversal is that, while women have learned to accept that they may need to support themselves, few women ever expect to support a husband and family, expect perhaps when their spouse dies unexpectedly. And while those working wives may intellectually understand and even appreciate that it is their at-home husbands who enable them to pursue their careers so aggressively, few of them ever accept this on a deep level. In our culture, it is still a relatively new phenomenon for women to provide for men; Pete believes that it just may not be in their wiring. Those women may experience a deep-seated struggle which, if left unchecked, can undermine the wife's respect for her husband and ultimately damage the marriage, sometimes irreparably.

Respect

Although Pete never lost his self-respect, for a time, he felt the loss of his wife's respect. She became judgmental and he became defensive about their positions in the marriage and in the world. And Pete is far from alone; many men report feeling this lack of respect, either self-respect or respect from others. This is especially true *early* in the role-reversed relationship, a particularly challenging time for most couples. Sometimes it manifests in idle comments from strangers or folks around the neighborhood, as we saw in Chapter 5 on stereotypes. Or the struggle may be mostly internal.

For Samuel, who we met in Chapter 2, it all seemed tied to issues of money. He says he wasn't even aware, at first, that he had voluntarily adopted an attitude that he was the supporting player, sort of a second-class citizen in his own household. He reports feeling a loss of self-esteem, a sort of emasculation, because his wife was paying the bills, which he translated to mean that he was not pulling his weight. In Samuel's case, the only one who didn't appreciate his efforts was Samuel.

But, like all of the successful couples profiled here, Samuel and Jeannie eventually found a solution. Once Samuel mapped out a career reentry plan, he could see the light at the end of the tunnel. It troubled him that he needed to identify so strongly with a career goal to feel his masculine power, but he also recognized that, for him, that was the reality. It was much better to acknowledge his feelings and adjust for them than to ignore them. Samuel also began to handle more of the family's finances and, although he says he feels a little silly admitting it, just putting his own credit card on the table instead of letting Jeannie pick up every check made him feel better. That small act of control added to his sense of personal power. Silly or not, it was his method of attitude adjustment, it worked, and he was sticking with it.

Flexibility

Almost every SAHD mentions flexibility as a key ingredient in making role reversal work. Most of the at-home dads who felt they were better suited to the parenting role than their spouses cited their flexibility, sense of humor, and ability to create order out of chaos—something they believed their working wives needed imposed upon them by the workplace—as vital parts of the whole.

Humor . . . and Good Humor

Humor has been known to cure diseases and heal broken hearts. And as every SAHD who's had to deal with colic, teething, or the terrible twos can tell you, daily doses of humor are an absolute necessity. Many at-home dads say that finding the humor in everyday situations can be a lifesaver, as well as an ongoing reminder of the joys of the job.

Mitch laughingly recalls the first time his four-year-old son, Sam, ever saw him in a business suit. An attorney turned at-home dad, Mitch was doing some volunteer fund-raising; as he bundled Sam into the car and headed for the baby-sitter's house, Sam asked his dad why he was wearing that strange outfit. "I have a meeting," Mitch told his son, "I'm going to work." Knowing a put-on when he heard it, Sam shot back, "Aww Dad, that's just for women!"

Keeping a sense of humor is also about finding the fun in the small moments. When Jay, the work-at-home web designer profiled in Chapter 2, was being interviewed for this book, he insisted on stopping in the middle of the interview for an ice cream break. It was the first time the Good Humor truck had ever pulled up in front of his house in a rural beachside community in Florida and, of course, it was imperative that he halt the interview so six-year-old Tucker could buy an ice cream. Like most SAHDs, Jay had his priorities in the right place and wasn't about to pass up that golden opportunity for fun—for him and Tucker. Once back to the interview, he was quick to note that it was his at-home status that allowed him the flexibility of having a job he loved *and* the opportunity to be there for Tucker's first Good Humor experience.

Perspective

Pete and Jessica found it crucial to maintain perspective and remember what was most important in their relationship. And what was most important to them was their daughter Josie's welfare and happiness. Perspective, a trait cultivated by all these courageous role reversers, is the ability to keep that greater goal in mind despite difficulties that will inevitably arise. When the going gets tough, you need the ability to look at yourselves and your relationship with a little objectivity—or to seek an objective opinion from a third party. Pete and Jessica worked through their issues of attitude, appreciation, and respect. Pete credits their deeper understanding to communication and a shared commitment to their daughter.

B Is for Balance

As Pete and Jessica planned their return to the United States, part of that process involved redirecting their family and career goals, and striking a balance they could both feel positive about. Balance is everything in making role reversal work. For couples who've traded traditional gender roles, modifying and personalizing those roles so marriage, career, and children are balanced is key. What working mom wants to put so much time and energy into her job that she barely has time for her kids? And what at-home dad plans to make his life revolve so fully around his children that he loses his skills, contacts, and power in the external world? "All or nothing" isn't what either of you is opting for. But how can you create and maintain the balance that is right for you?

Balance by Teamwork

Hogan's secret for creating the right balance is "Don't keep score." In other words, you and your spouse are a team, but don't expect everything to always be equal. It's not a contest to see either who does the most, or who owes the most. And Hogan should know. He and Tina face special challenges because their son Wesley is disabled. Taking care of Wesley, and making sure their other two sons, Grant and Matt, get plenty of love, time, and attention is a full-time job. It's also very much a team effort.

Celebrating the holidays with her family is very important to Tina. Hogan makes sure that he sets aside the time to care for Wesley, so that his wife can spend some well-deserved leisure hours with their other sons and her parents. For Hogan, an extraordinarily involved and loving father, this is not a hardship. He cherishes his time alone with Wesley, and also dearly wants to give Tina the opportunity to have her needs met, as she does his. This is the gift of teamwork that Tina and Hogan give each other.

Even though strangers or casual acquaintances are frequently at a loss as to what to say about their special situation, Tina and Hogan are acutely aware of the demands facing them. They know that many couples with disabled children end up in divorce, so they are extremely attentive to and protective of their marriage, just as they are of their children. While Tina, Grant, and Matt spend some holiday time with her family, Hogan willingly stays home with Wesley. But rather than expecting to be paid back in equal time, Hogan just accepts this arrangement as something that Tina needs and that he is more than willing to give. Tina carries her weight in many other ways, but neither spouse expects equal payback for their efforts. For them, keeping score would not only be pointless, it would be unthinkable.

Joann and Jay have found a formula for teamwork that definitely works for them. Joann is a behavioral psychologist who works outside the home. Jay is, of course, the "good humored" web designer and mastermind behind Slowlane.com, the online lifesaver for SAHDs. The work-family balance he and Joann have built, has, despite a few sleep-deprived moments, given them an incredible foundation to raise their son and pursue two challenging careers simultaneously. Of course, it doesn't happen all at once. While Joann was working full-time and supporting the family as a psychologist specializing in pain management, Jay was raising Tucker and building his web business. As Jay's two babies, Tucker and the web business, both began to mature, Jay began to devote more time to work until he had a full-time home-based business. Meantime, Joann began to condense her full-time work schedule into a four-day week. She and Jay had found a balance in the middle. Best of all, Tucker still comes first. He has been raised by his parents full-time since the day he was born.

Balance by Battling Isolation

Isolation is cited as one of the biggest challenges facing at-home dads. And, as the word suggests, they usually face it completely alone. Working wives, with their overstressed, overscheduled lives, often long for a little solitude. But let's not confuse alone time, a necessity for every parent, at home or not, with isolation. Isolation is not a weekend alone in a mountain cabin. It's being the only adult within earshot of a screaming toddler, a beeping microwave, and a barking dog. Isolation is a scourge to all housebound parents, but especially to networking-challenged at-home dads.

But the dads we've met all had words of wisdom about fighting it. Some did say that isolation was not a problem for them, or that it was a problem only in the beginning of their at-home tenure, but all recognized it as a potential issue for SAHDs. Barry, an at-home father of two and part-time public relations consultant, succinctly summed up the advice most gave: "Get up, get dressed, get out!"

For Barry, this meant having breakfast in the local coffee shop with his two children most mornings. For others, it meant errands, play groups, or sporting activity. Anything to get kids and Dad out of the house and mingling with other kids and dads—or moms, as is generally the case. Most SAHDs had their own methods of infiltrating at-home-mom circles—asking the neighbors over so the kids can have a play date while the grown-ups get acquainted over coffee; volunteering at school or Brownies. Whatever it takes. But our savvy SAHDs also learned that meeting at-home moms on an emotional level really turned the corner for them.

What these dads learned was to recognize that, as uncomfortable as they were getting to know the at-home moms in their neighborhood, the moms were often just as uncomfortable with them. The balance in a group shifted when a man joined in the discussion. It didn't matter if the discussion was about stocks or sports—yes, women do occasionally discuss those things—or about breastfeeding or the latest episode of Sex in the City. There was now a gender issue. Most dads acknowledged it and moved past it. Some joked about it. One dad reports finally being treated like—then labeled as—a "girlfriend" among his mom pals. And he was wise enough to recognize that as a badge of honor and a rite of passage.

Of course, seeking out other dads, particularly other stay-at-home dads, is a great antidote to isolation. There's nothing like shared experience to create an instant bond. For some dads who live in more remote areas, that bond may exist only online or via telephone. For others, there are at-home-dad groups, some that include the kids, some that are adults-only escapes from the kids. Stay-at-home dads need to remember to, literally and figuratively, get up, get dressed, and get out!

Balance by Maintaining Outside Interests

Let's get back to Pete, a true innovator among stay-at-home dads. While Pete is the first to admit that he is hardly driven by commercial success and is comfortable with the fact that Jessica easily out-earns him, he has wisely kept a balance between caring for Josie and keeping up his career skills. As a part-time designer, Pete works several jobs a month, charging competitive professional rates for his talents. Most of the money goes right back into his business, either for equipment or materials, but, to Pete, the important thing is keeping up his skills, his confidence, and his contacts. Design is his creative outlet and his personal passion. And keeping abreast with his competitors ensures that, should he decide to return to graphics design full-time, he will be ready.

And what about Jay, who modified his entire business plan when he and Joann found out that Tucker was on the way? Jay had planned to launch a full-scale marketing and web design business, but when they found out Joann was pregnant, he modified that plan. What Jay didn't do is abandon or indefinitely postpone it. He just turned his endeavor into a *home-based* business, so he could care for Tucker and launch his company at the same time. In hindsight, Jay says he might have slowed down the business a bit so he didn't miss out on five years of sleep. But then, Bill Laut quips, he would have had his triplets one at a time if nature had only accommodated him: Balance doesn't always work out exactly as you want it to. The point to remember is that all these innovative at-homers understood that they needed outlets beyond their children and outside their families, whenever and whatever was right for them in their particular situation.

C Is for Communication

As a SAHD/WM couple facing multiple challenges, you've got to become exceptionally effective communicators by whatever means are available to you, including trial and error. If you think marriage is tough, or raising kids is a challenge, try marriage *and* children *and* role reversal. Now try it in a vacuum, where you and your spouse are hesitant to discuss tough issues openly and honestly. You're going to be fighting an uphill battle all the way unless you learn to talk to each other with candor and compassion, every day.

But communication isn't just about spouse-to-spouse dialogue, although that's where it starts for the purposes of our parent-focused perspective. Let's also look at how we talk to and about our children, as well as how we communicate globally—that is, to the outside world—about our unique family structures.

Couples Communication

Jim, whom we've already met, is an outspoken and passionate former social services director turned full-time at-home caregiver to his two young children, Lauren and Gabriel. Jim's wife, Leslie, is a dynamic and successful electronics engineer. The evolution from their early days as a two-career couple to their current status as a SAHD/WM family—a switch Jim terms his "career change"—poignantly illustrates the supreme importance of communication in this transformational process.

Although they knew it would not always be easy, Jim and Leslie were committed from the start to communicating openly with each other. Jim credits their participation in the Roman Catholic Marriage Encounter program with providing the couple with good basic communication tools. He and Leslie learned how to talk about highly charged emotional issues and, key to their communicative process as a couple, how to identify who felt more passionately about a specific circumstance or decision. If one feels more passionately than the other, by definition they don't have the same level of concern. Once any issue was brought to light and clearly articulated on both sides, they were better able to make informed decisions that addressed each partner's concerns and took into appropriate account the more passionate point of view.

Of course, good communication doesn't happen magically overnight, and issues don't always get resolved immediately. And that's exactly what Jim discovered when he realized just how unhappy he was with Lauren's daycare situation. Not that the daycare was bad; in fact, it was very good private care in a neighborhood caregiver's home. It just wasn't parental care. As Jim's dissatisfaction grew, he expressed it to Leslie. But she could not see how they could possibly afford to give up Jim's income and live on one salary so he could stay home. Her income was substantially higher than his, but they lived in an expensive Southern California neighborhood and Leslie was convinced they had to remain a two-wage couple, at least for the foreseeable future.

But Jim persisted, seeking out like-minded people—these were few and far between—with whom he could discuss his feelings and find support. One such person was his assistant, who had been an at-home mom raising her seven children until a divorce forced her, reluctantly, back into the workplace. Further fueling his determination to become a full-time parent was Jim's increasing sense of hypocrisy. As a social services director, overseeing numerous programs including a large homeless shelter, Jim often advocated for quality childcare and for parents to be able to be home with their children, even though that was a relatively atypical position for an administrator to adopt at that time.

Yet, here he was having someone else take care of his own child for ten or eleven hours a day so he could help other people lead better lives. The irony finally became too much for him, and he told Leslie one of them would have to stay home to care for Lauren. He didn't care who it was, but he was convinced their daughter needed a full-time parent at home. And, clearly the more passionate one in this particular matter, Jim was determined to win Leslie over.

Still, Leslie was rightfully concerned about the family's finances, so Jim sought out additional counseling through an Employee Assistance Program that he himself had implemented. The sage counselor gave Jim what he still considers an amazing piece of advice. We told the story in Chapter 4: the counselor suggested that Jim add up all the expenses that would be eliminated by full-time parental care and see just how far his salary really stretched. When Jim showed Leslie that, after all work- and kid-related expenses, he was bringing home a minuscule $5,000, it became obvious that he should stay home. So, after wrapping up a number of programs and hiring the appropriate replacement for himself, Jim finally effected his career transition and became a full-time stay-at-home dad. Now that's a commitment to ongoing communication!

Kid Communication

Another oft-repeated method of spouse-to-spouse communication centers around the children. For detail-starved moms who fear they are missing out on the special moments of childhood to which their at-home husbands are privy, many SAHDs have made a special commitment to become the official archivists, videographers, and family historians. After all, people decide not to put the kids in daycare or leave them at home with a nanny partly because they want to watch them grow up, moment to moment. For the working mom who must live those moments vicariously, every photo, video, and kid-constructed heirloom preserved by a loving at-home dad is like gold.

Human resources consultant Lori—wife of Barry of "Get up,

get dressed, get out" wisdom—sums up a common concern of breadwinner moms. She finds that most of the sharing about the day's activities for her two kids, Christina and Bradford, seems to happen right after school and not over dinner, when she is there to partake. And though she understands that as her children grow, they take on their own friends and interests, the task of relaying the intimate details of her children's lives often falls to her husband.

Many working moms are grateful to their spouses for keeping them up-to-date on all the big and little moments of their children's lives. Dad's reporting can, of course, take many different forms, depending on his technical skill and available equipment. Many SAHDs enjoy making videotapes of special and everyday events for their wives—school activities, parties, silly moments at home. Often, Mom is there for key moments; but when she's not, Dad fills the gap.

My husband, Ned, an at-home dad to our two boys, is the keeper of the baby books. (Now that the boys are past preschool and a little put off by their books being labeled as "babies," these are officially called the "Memory Books.") They hold everything, from the label of the first acceptable jar of baby vegetables, to scraps of favorite shirts, to movie-ticket stubs, to vacation memorabilia. Ned takes his responsibility as archivist very seriously and, lest all these little bits and pieces of daily existence get out of hand and become unclassifiable, he labels them meticulously.

Many of the SAHDs/WMs profiled in this book say they've been asked a million times what they tell their kids about their role reversal. Most of them have the same answer. They simply explain that their children are so important that Mom and Dad arranged their family life so one of them, Dad, could be there to love and care for them full-time. This is immediately understood and accepted by even the youngest child.

And when parents teach their kids about how their role-reversal decision was made and explain that they are living the consequences, they also teach them—consciously or not—how to make decisions for themselves. Jim tells a story about the time Lauren was invited to two birthday parties at exactly the same time.

Although she begged him to tell her whether she should attend the party of the family friend or that of her girlfriend from school, he refused to help her. It would be a tough decision, he told her, but one she would have to make on her own and then live with. Lauren learned a lot about friendship, compromise, and living with the consequences of a decision when she devised a plan that allowed her to attend her girlfriend's party, then join the family friends for a postparty dinner. This is a kid who stands to learn a lot from her parents. And because they walk the walk, she's listening.

Global Communication

Sadly, many at-home dads report that they've had difficulty communicating with some working dads because of the differences inherent in their status. They say it's not so much that they're not up on their financial news or sports stats—though many did profess greater knowledge of the Cub Scouts than the Chicago Cubs. Rather, the SAHDs found themselves something of an oddity at parties and social gatherings, to say nothing of their wives' business functions, because they actually *liked to* talk about their children. They could tell funny stories about what their kids said at school or did on the soccer field. And the other dads—the full-time working dads—just couldn't relate. The at-homers often said they'd have been more comfortable in the kitchen with the moms. And they didn't care—they knew that they were more involved in and more passionate about their children's lives, growth, and happiness than anything else on the planet. Many of those dads—*both the at-home and the breadwinning variety*—felt a profound sense of loss for any dad who would never experience the joy of raising his kids first-hand.

On the other hand, not satisfied with the status quo, many of the trailblazing role reversers are out there taking their communication skills public, talking to the world about their unusual lifestyles. They chat online, they publish newsletters, they design websites, they teach seminars. In the back of this book you'll find a listing of some of these resources, many created and maintained by the dads themselves. But there are other, uniquely personal ways these parents communicate their message to a broader audience, including those who are unfamiliar with the lifestyle.

Several innovative dads, including both Hogan and Jim, have turned their full-time at-home fathering roles into part-time fathering businesses. Hogan teaches his Proud Dad seminars in corporate settings, demonstrating to working dads how to be involved and loving fathers. Jim established a program through a local hospital to teach expectant fathers how to care for babies. Both of these pioneering dads decided to take their personal perspective on involved fathering and their innate talent for communication to a broader audience so that dads and expectant dads could benefit from the wealth of their knowledge. Whether any of their students become at-home dads is irrelevant. What they will become, thanks to Jim and Hogan's shared insights, are better fathers.

On a truly global level, Pete, the at-home dad who followed his working wife to Taiwan, gives regular presentations to Taiwanese parents and healthcare workers about his unique lifestyle. Although the SAHD/WM model is much more common in the United States and other parts of the world, such as Scandinavia, than it is in Taiwan, Pete has drawn enormous interest from Taiwanese couples. He is an ambassador, spreading the word about the challenges and the joys of stay-at-home dads everywhere.

But no one sums up the success and significance of the stay-at-home dad experience as poignantly as Chris, a SAHD from Wake Forest, North Carolina. Chris is a real mold-breaker among mold-breaking dads. A former teacher whose imposing physique is offset by his gentle demeanor, Chris is a stay-at-home dad to his pre-school son and daughter.

As we've seen, at-homers regularly swap stories, exchange childcare tips, and share experiences through the grassroots SAHD network, linked by online sites like Slowlane.com and by the annual At-Home Dads Convention, but Chris took this support and community further than most when he was diagnosed with testicular cancer. He was a favorite at the dads' convention held in suburban Chicago every fall; when he missed a conference because he was fighting for his life, the SAHD community rallied around him with prayers, support, and—what else—a flood of e-mails.

After chemotherapy and several surgeries, Chris's illness went into remission. Counting his blessings, he returned to the next at-home-dads convention to spend time with his friends and colleagues. Wrapping up the weekend conference, this soft-spoken, powerful, six-foot-two, 230-pound dad thanked his fellow SAHDs for their outpouring of love and, as his voice cracked and tears welled up in his eyes, told them that every day as his feet hit the floor—even on Mondays, usually the toughest in his household—he was thankful for the decision he had made to stay home with his children. Thankful for every day he'd already spent caring for them and for every moment yet to come. If there was anything his experience had taught him, Chris told the roomful of enraptured dads, it was how meaningful a dad's presence was to his children, and he hoped all the stay-at-home dads everywhere realized how blessed—and how brave—they were for the commitment they were living one moment at a time.

Quick Review

Every family faces childcare challenges. SAHD/WM couples, with their unique lifestyle structure, just face a few more than most. This chapter details some of those specific situations and how a handful of pioneering parents handled them.

The ABCs of SAHD/WM life.

- A is for *Attitude*. SAHD/WMs couples—like Bill and Sheila, parents of toddler triplets, or Pete and Jessica, who moved halfway around the world with their daughter—say they couldn't have successfully rewritten their parenting roles if they didn't have the right attitude, including appreciation, respect, flexibility, a sense of humor, and the ability to keep things in perspective.

- *B* is for *Balance*. Every couple finds the right balance for their family. For Hogan and Tina, it's by learning to meet one another's needs without keeping score. For Jay and Joann, it's all about teamwork, which is the only way they could have ever launched a family and two careers at the same time. For Barry, it was all about refusing to give into isolation by getting out into the world and pursuing outside interests, while Lori was away at work.

- *C* is for *Communication*. All these SAHD/WM couples have had to learn to become expert communicators, like Jim and Leslie who redefined their family to honor their values. Some dads, including Jim, Hogan, and Pete, have taken their gifts as communicators to the outside world to teach others about the joys, as well as the frustrations, of the SAHD/WM lifestyle.

SAHDs are living their commitment moment by moment.

Chris summed up his stay-at-home-dad experience with true poignancy when, after successfully battling cancer, he acknowledged all SAHDs at the recent At-Home Dad Convention. "I hope all the stay-at-home dads everywhere," he told the group, "realize how blessed and brave they are for the commitment they are living one moment at a time."

Chapter 10

Tips from the Trenches

A nd now, perhaps the most important chapter of all. Here's a survival guide from the guys who really know: the stay-at-home dads themselves. They've divulged their tricks, tools, and tips on home and childcare that you can duplicate or adapt to your family's specific needs. And because SAHD's are known for their generosity, this chapter will reveal their hard-earned knowledge, shortcuts, and secrets. And it will definitely prove that sometimes dads do things a little differently!

Not So Basic Childcare

Diapers: Where It All Starts . . . and Ends

- Make the dirtiest job a little fun—but don't let your wife see this one. Toss a well-wrapped dirty diaper across the nursery into the diaper pail eight to ten times a day for two and a half years. You'll be amazed by how your free-throw average improves.
- Bait and switch. Hand the baby a clean diaper (toy, diaper

wipe box) as a distraction while he's on the changing table. He'll squirm less and cut the changing time in half.

- Stock up! Go to your local warehouse store and load up the minivan. *Don't ever run out of diapers!*
- Keep diapers stashed in the car trunk and at Grandma's. You won't have to deplete your precious diaper bag supply—and you'll be prepared for extreme emergencies like snowstorms.
- Put fabric softener sheets in the bottom of the diaper pail. They'll combat that toxic waste odor.

Diapering on the Go

- No changing table in sight? Why struggle with the seat of the car like the moms do? Stay-at-home dads find that a clean, carpeted car trunk does the trick. It's level, the baby can't fall out, and, bonus, there's plenty of space to keep all the baby gear close at hand.
- Keep a small toxic waste kit under the stroller, in your backpack, or in a small fannypack with a couple of diapers, some wipes in a zipper bag, an almost-empty tube of diaper rash cream, and a nonperishable snack. No need to haul around that huge diaper bag packed with rarely used items like a change of clothes, blankets, and just-in-case medicines. Leave the big bag in the car for when the major diaper blowouts occur. They will.

Potty Training Made Easier

- One fiber-loving dad found an extremely creative way to potty-train his reluctant three-year-old. A couple of times a day, he'd throw a handful of Cheerios in the toilet bowl so his son could use them for tinkle target practice. It wasn't long before Dad could *adios* the Cheerios—or at least find another use for them—and his son would use the potty sans cereal.

- Overalls are the kiss of death. Pants for the boys and dresses for the girls until the potty is mastered.
- Pre–potty training tip for SAHDs of boys: Hold your son while you pee. Let him see how it works.
- Make a sticker chart. Reward your child with a sticker every time he goes in the toilet. Kids love to see how proud you are and how fast their sticker collection grows.
- Try "big boy" or "big girl" underwear with a diaper or pull-ups over them. The undies will get wet, providing the desired discomfort level, while the diapers will prevent leakage so there's less mess for you to clean up.
- Dads, when your little girl's got to go, look for public locations that offer "family restrooms." If those aren't available, announce that a little girl will be coming into the men's room with her father. This gives anyone using the urinal a chance to finish up and clear out. Some dads know all their local restrooms by heart.
- When your daughter's old enough to try the ladies' room alone, stand at the door and talk to her until she's finished. She'll be comforted by your presence, and you'll be comforted knowing she's safe.

Comfort

- Buy your child's favorite comfort item in multiples. If it's a blankie or a stuffed animal, get four or five in case you lose one. Keep a backup in the trunk and bring an extra security object along on vacation, just in case.

Emergencies/Medical Problems

- Post the number for your local poison control center by all your phones. And keep it in your wallet in case your kid decides to eat berries off a bush in the park.
- Act quickly. Find a person in charge. "One time my son dis-

appeared in Target. I was picking out shoes for him and looked down for a moment and he was gone. I grabbed security. They closed off all the entrances immediately. We found my son safely playing in the toy department."

- Wear a fanny pack with often-needed emergency items. One well-prepared SAHD reports, "My daughter has asthma, but she's too young to carry a purse. I started wearing a fanny pack to keep her emergency inhaler on me at all times. I can pull it out quickly without fumbling through a backpack or diaper bag. It's scary for her, but she knows I'm always prepared."
- Cut a wad of tissues in half with scissors. When kids get colds, they can go through a box of tissues in no time. This way, you get twice the mileage, with tissues the perfect kid size, too.
- "Prevention is the key. Get your flu shot, wash your hands often, eat healthy, and exercise," says one savvy SAHD. "I'm upset when the kids are sick, but it's even worse if I come down with the flu. You don't get a sick day on the couch when you're in charge of the kids."

Money, Money, Money

- It's never too early to start saving for your baby's future. Even if it's a little bit of money, start some sort of college fund. Have the grandparents put money into the fund instead of buying some insanely expensive toy. You'll be thankful later on, when that fund grows and grows.
- Give your kids a moderate allowance. They can save it to be used for anything they want. "Visits to the market or the toy store are finally tolerable. They still beg me to buy them something, but now I tell them they can spend all their allowance or save it for something else. It makes them think and it gets me off the hook."
- Use cash once in a while. Let your kids pay at the register or figure the tip or total at a restaurant. They'll learn about making change, counting, and the concept of money—a lost notion in this age of credit and ATM cards.

Everyday Stuff

- Let them explore the house, as long as it's safe and supervised. They'll lose interest when it's no longer taboo. One father let his nine-month-old play with the electric sockets. "I had installed the safety covers so I knew they were safe. My son tried to get them open. He was fascinated with them . . . for about five minutes. I didn't say a word, and he lost interest. He's never looked at them since."
- Keep a disposable camera in the diaper bag/backpack/car at all times. Use it for your Kodak moments or let the kids amuse themselves by learning to take pictures.
- Use potato-chip-bag clips to attach a light blanket over your stroller to block out the sun.
- Shoes and socks go on best when the baby is in the stroller, high chair, or car seat. You'll save time and effort instead of wrestling with your baby or toddler.
- Always remember: everything takes five to seven times longer than you think it will!

Discipline

When Good Kids Go Bad

- Give warnings before you issue the time-outs. Give them a chance to modify the behavior, without diluting the effectiveness of the time-outs.
- As kids get older, "separate them from the herd before disciplining." A private discussion is more meaningful and causes less embarrassment for both of you when an unacceptable behavior needs to be addressed.
- Pick your battles. "If they want to wear shorts and it's cold outside, the worst that can happen is they'll freeze their tushes off." If you fight all the small battles, your life will be a nightmare.

Accentuate the Positive

- Create a daily journal of your kid's successes: taking a nap, eating dinner, using the potty, cleaning their room. At the end of the day, let them choose stickers to put in their books next to each entry. This offsets a lot of time-outs and reinforces the positive.
- Limit Internet surfing and TV watching by using a reward system. Chart surfing and watching habits in terms of length and types of sites and shows watched. Choose an agreed-upon amount and have the kids stick to the plan. Offer bonus time or coveted toys and activities when limits are kept.

Housecleaning

General Tips

- Kids love to help, even toddlers. Let them sort silverware from the dishwasher, dust, and sweep floors. Enlist their help before you actually need it. It may be more work for you, but it will serve you well in the long run.
- And when they're too young to help, let them think they're helping anyway. Give the little ones a spray bottle of water or a polishing cloth, so they think they're cleaning right along with Dad. They can't hurt anything, but they can learn a lot about responsibility.
- The best way to avoid dealing with it is to deal with it—whatever *it* is. When it's done you won't have to deal with it anymore.
- Strap your baby in a bouncy seat or stroller (yes, inside the house!) to keep him safe from toxic cleaning chemicals. It's also an easy way to bring him from room to room with you while you clean.
- Clean where the kids are playing. If they want to play in the garage, do laundry—or deal with whatever else is lurking in your garage. If they want to hang out in the living room, dust

or vacuum there. And if there's no work to be done where they want to play, lucky you. Join in the fun.

- Every so often drag the high chair outside and hose it down.
- Every so often put all the plastic toys through a cycle in the dishwasher.
- If you run out of *laundry* detergent, don't ever, ever, ever put *dishwashing* liquid in the washing machine.
- Do it now. Don't let stuff pile up. It'll only get worse.
- Make the beds every morning. It will make you feel you got something done that day.
- Many dads offered some variation on this theme: "Do what's most important to your wife. If her thing is a clean bathroom, spend your time on the bathroom. Find out her pet peeves and go there first so she doesn't see the glaring bad stuff and overlook all the good stuff you did all day."
- Use an industrial strength shop-vac (the heavy-duty professional vacuum used by builders—it sucks up both wet and dry). You can even vacuum the kids in their high chairs after really messy meals.

Lessons in Laundry

- Wash all the new baby clothes and bedding before you go to the hospital to have the baby. The first weeks home are the craziest, and laundry will be the last thing you'll want to do.
- Another favored method: *avoid* laundry. Buy multiples of things you'll use often in those early weeks and months: burp cloths, baby bunting sleepers, pajamas (yours).
- Put burping cloths under new babies in their cribs or bassinets or in your bed. That way you won't have to change all the sheets when they spit up or blow out their diapers.
- Keep a burping cloth hanging from your rear pants pocket like a handkerchief at all times. Burps happen. Burps happen often.
- Early on, you'll probably do laundry every day. As the baby gets older, try to pick one or two days a week to do laundry. You'll feel less postal.

- Have your wife put hand washables and dry-clean-onlys in a separate location from the regular laundry. This prevents having to read labels or doing permanent damage to a silk blouse.

Food Tips

Cooking

- Wake up and smell the formula, moms. The kitchen is no longer yours.
- The microwave is quite possibly the most significant invention since the wheel. Some raw materials, a few taps on the keypad, and you've got dinner. Be grateful. Be very grateful.
- Salad-in-a-bag is the second most significant invention. A bag of greens, some dressing, a pair of scissors, and you've got your sides.
- When you're on a cooking roll, make two meals at once and freeze one for later.
- Keep a continuous grocery list going. Make sure everyone adds to it. Stick to the list. No impulse purchases like sugared cereals or squishy blue foods.
- Concentrate on foods you can pre-prepare. "We eat a lot of noodle dishes," says one cooking-challenged SAHD. "They're easy and it looks like you did a lot of work, but you didn't really."
- Add food coloring to less popular foods and the kids may even eat them. They have a huge affinity for the disgusting.
- Who delivers in your neighborhood? Keep a folder by the phone. Even if you're anti-takeout, there may be times you'll need it. Be prepared.
- Your attempt at animal-shaped pancakes a failure? Have the kids guess what they are. It fuels their imagination and their tummies.
- When the kids are helping in the kitchen, don't worry about

the mess—but don't let your wife in the kitchen, either, because she *will* worry about the mess.

- Avoid ice-pop messes. Cut a slit in a small paper plate and poke the stick through. Drips are caught in the plate.
- Freeze the long ice-pop sticks, then cut them in half. The kids eat half the sugar and it saves you from the futile attempt to rip the plastic open every time.
- Get the kids fed and out the door to school with less hassle by making a breakfast meal plan in advance. Have the kids choose a food and beverage for each day of the week. They'll love planning it. And as soon as they're old enough, let them fix their own breakfast.
- Zipper-style plastic bags should be bought in massive quantities. Snacks, frozen meals, lunches, toys, wipes—everything goes in them. Buy them in all the sizes available.
- The pizza delivery guy is not necessarily your new best friend. (See "Losing the Pregnancy Weight," below.)

Eating (Dining Comes Later) in Restaurants

- When you sit down at the table, order spoons by the half-dozen. Babies love to play with them.
- Order ice water. Add spoons. Teething babies love the cold on their gums, and they'll be entertained for minutes.
- Asian restaurants have great soup spoons. Teething babies really love the wide bowls and fancy designs. And, of course, there are lots of things with noodles.
- Always, always have Cheerios with you.
- Tip the busboys well if you want to be welcome in the restaurant again.
- Portable booster seats that double as carrying cases are the greatest invention, and they don't have the previous kid's syrup on them.
- To prevent frequent clothing changes or stains, make a larger bib: cut a hole big enough for the baby's head in a large dish

towel or bath towel. May not be a fashion statement, but it'll do the job.

- Wipe down the high chair (or booster seat) with diaper wipes before the baby goes in. The restaurant probably doesn't hose down its high chairs the way you do.
- Individually packaged antibacterial wipes are great to keep in your pocket in case strangers touch your baby's hands, and before meals in restaurants. You can inconspicuously wipe their hands off. Diaper wipes work well, too.

Personal Hygiene—His!

- Shower while they nap.
- Shower before your wife leaves for work.
- Shower or bathe with them (until it's no longer age-appropriate).
- Shower every day.
- Shave every day.
- Put on clean clothes, socks, and underwear every day. Even though yesterday's sweats seem clean, just don't do it.

Losing the Pregnancy Weight—His!

- Dig out the gym equipment. Read the sports section on the StairMaster or treadmill while they nap. It's amazing what a moment to yourself will do for your brain and your body.
- No matter how tempting your kids' meals are, don't finish them. Ever.
- The television is not your friend. Get off the couch as quickly as possible.
- Wear a belt. It's a constant reminder of your former waistline.
- Wear pants, not sweats; otherwise you'll keep expanding.
- Start doing abs before the baby gets too heavy. They go from

seven to twenty-five pounds in one year. Your back will kill you if you don't have strong abs.
- Jogging strollers are a necessity.
- They can run faster than you can get in shape. Start now.

Guy Gear and Dad Duds

The Stuff That Works

- Clothing—like life—should never be all black or all white. Black clothing shows the gunk, poop, and spit all too well. White clothing attracts the technicolor food groups—beets, berries, strained peaches, etc.
- Dads prefer a black or navy diaper bag (Peter Rabbit and Winnie-the-Pooh just don't cut it). Backpacks work even better for a lot of dads.
- Buy a baby swing.
- Cup holders are a very nice little accessory for your stroller, too.
- Chest-mounted baby carriers, in the early months while the baby's still light, leave both hands free for shopping, vacuuming, talking on the phone. No cooking or dangerous household work while you're wearing one, though!

Family Organization

Some General Rules

- Try to eat breakfast and dinner together as a family at the dining room table. It will anchor all of you. Schedule activities around this family time. Try not to let anything like soccer practice or late meetings or evening television cut into this precious activity. Be flexible, but make sure you build in some sacrosanct family dinner times.

- Even though you are a stay-at-home dad and your wife works out of the home, claim some traditional mommy and daddy functions if you feel the need. Daddy mows the lawn or Mommy sews the Halloween costumes. Some things never change and don't have to.

- Assign chores and give allowances based on successful completion of tasks. Ask for help unloading groceries or doing yardwork. You can't do it all by yourself, and this is a reminder that everyone has to help out to make the family function.

Scheduling/Juggling/Sharing

- Nap time is Dad's work time. Plan to use that little window every day. You never know how long it will be, but be prepared to seize it, whether to pay bills or shower (or take a nap yourself).

- Stick to your schedule. "The hardest part of the day is from dinnertime to bedtime," one SAHD told me, "especially if my wife isn't home yet or has a late meeting scheduled. Everyone is melting down then. We have rigid bedtime rituals. The only way to survive this time of the day is to stay on your schedule."

- Think of yourself as the family administrator. Most SAHDs aren't just taking care of the children. They are running the entire household, often including their wives' nonwork lives. Be prepared to think of yourself in those terms.

- Put the family calendar on the refrigerator. Make sure everybody updates it and synchs it with their own. Especially Mom. Every week. No exceptions.

- Buy a cordless phone with a headset. You can actually talk and change diapers at the same time—really.

- Let the machine answer the phone. You need to control your time as much as you can. Save yourself that forty-seventh telemarketing call of the day.

- Carve out some downtime every day, even if it's just five minutes alone in the john.

- When you add home maintenance chores, such as plumbing, painting, or yardwork (things most men do on weekends), to the 24/7 stay-at-home-dad responsibilities, the job is enormous. Consider hiring professionals for things you used to tackle yourself. Even if you could do it for less, the expense is worth it. Hang on to the jobs you actually enjoy and farm out the ones you dread.
- Dads, do everything you can to include your wife without actually demanding her time. Make her videos and photos so she's always included in everything. Send her faxes and e-mails during the day. Keep notes so you won't forget something. At the risk of falling prey to a stereotype, most women like details.
- Much of the sharing with school-aged children occurs right after school, before Mom gets home. Make sure to bring up the subjects again at dinner to get her up to speed. Or let her create a special game designed to get kids beyond one-word answers, like asking them to rate different things that happened to them during the day on a 1-to-10 scale, game show style. Or asking the kids to relate a highlight/lowlight of each day's activities and having the grown-ups do the same.

School/Homework/Learning

- Make sure all school events are posted on the family calendar on the fridge.
- When scheduling school events, allow for transportation time, locker room time, and post-event chatter. Nothing ends exactly on the dot.
- Sometimes only one of you will be able to attend a function. Discuss with your children which are the most important events to attend. Include them in the decision-making process. Trade off on which parent attends which events.
- To limit morning madness, make lunches the night before. Or buy the school lunch program. Believe it or not, most school cafeterias have improved dramatically since you were a kid.

- Make sure sports uniforms, musical instruments, science projects, "show-and-tell" stuff, special treats, homework, and permission slips are organized the night before.
- Remember that dads can be great room helpers, too! And volunteering in your kids' classroom sends him or her the message that school is important.
- Don't overbook your kids. "We let our sons choose one activity a semester," says a wise SAHD. "It can be a sport, a band, or a club activity. Schoolwork and family life are important and get lost with too many outside activities. Kids need downtime and unorganized play time, too. They can't get that when they have four sports, three clubs, and two lessons every week."
- Keep to the homework plan. "Homework can be a real bear. When Mommy gets home the kids want her time, and she wants to play with them, but if we don't get homework started right after dinner, they don't finish until way past their bedtime. The same issue pops up on weekends. Keep to the plan. That way, kids understand that they're following a prescribed plan, and it's not about you being the bad guy every day."
- Even though you're doing an excellent job caring for your child, don't be ashamed to compare your child's development to that of his peers. Tutors and specialists exist for a reason. "I had my son in a play group in the neighborhood. He didn't seem to be talking at the same level as kids his age. Turns out he needed speech therapy on a weekly basis for a few months. Now he's doing fine, but I keep thinking, What if he had been in daycare or with the nanny? Would they have recognized that he wasn't communicating like his peers? Would the problem have gotten worse?"

Family Rituals and Holidays

- Remember the true meaning of the holidays. "The kids understand that sometimes holidays happen while Mommy's working at the hospital. Luckily, due to a very diversified staff, when possible, the doctors trade off for holidays that are important for their own religion. If the holiday is important enough for us to celebrate, and Mommy just can't be there, we'll do it on another day when all of us can be together. Christmas is still Christmas to us, even if it is December 27 sometimes."

- Discuss what's important to the family. No use killing yourself to prepare Aunt Bertha's recipe if nobody really eats it at Thanksgiving anyway. Prioritize how you want to spend the holidays so your wife doesn't overcompensate and you don't feel overwhelmed trying to execute the "perfect" holiday.

- Take behind-the-scenes photos for your wife of all special occasions. "One of our favorite photos was of our four-year-old son getting fitted for a tux for his aunt's wedding. Better than any of the professional wedding photos."

- Come up with creative ways to give yourself a holiday break. "Even though we usually have a big party that weekend, our son gets to spend the night of his actual birthday at Grandma and Grandpa's. The three of them go out to eat or play games. It's a win-win for my wife and me because we get a night off with no guilt and are reminded why he has a birthday in the first place."

Vacations

Dad's

- Take a dad vacation! "All year I look forward to it. One weekend a year, a bunch of my old buddies go away for a golf weekend. We drink beer, smoke cigars, play poker. All the guy stuff. By the last night I'm missing my wife and the kids. I don't need another fix until the next year."

The Whole Family's

- On long flights, it's worth it to buy your infant a seat and keep the baby in the FAA-approved strap-in seat. Separate seats are required for kids over two, but are preferable for all kids, regardless of age, for their safety and your comfort. It's not a vacation if either of you is holding a squirming or sleeping baby the whole flight. It's exhausting and impossible to eat. You'll thank yourself later. Just book early, so you don't have to pay full fare.
- Childproof your hotel room by putting plants and decorative items away in the closet. Bring your own electric socket covers. That way toddlers and kids can explore without your hovering every second.
- Theme parks can actually make for a good vacation, since they cater to kids and families. Have a game plan so you maintain parental sanity, and don't try to cram in too much.
- Suite-style hotels work great. They are often affordable and have refrigerators, stoves, microwaves, and, best of all, a separate bedroom for Mom and Dad!
- Don't be surprised if Mom and Dad need a vacation after the family vacation is over.

Entertainment

Kids'

- Find out something your kid loves and do it often. "When my son was little he used to love to ride elevators. We found this mall that had great elevators, and we'd actually have outings to that mall and ride the elevators all day. He couldn't have been happier, it was free, and I occasionally even got a few errands done while we were there."
- Expand your child's musical horizons. "I couldn't handle listening to the syrupy-sweet purple dinosaur any longer. I put on my classic rock. I thought I had died and gone to heaven

when my three-year-old daughter was standing in the drive-
way teaching the neighborhood kids lyrics from Queen."

- Make play a priority. On his deathbed, no father ever said, "I
  should have dusted more often." Get on the floor and play
  with your kids. They'll remember that their whole lives.
- Tupperware containers, cardboard boxes, laundry baskets,
  and paper are the cheapest and best-loved toys.
- Clean paint brushes and buckets of water provide minutes of
  fun. Let them "paint" the house while you do yardwork.
- Bubbles. Never forget bubbles.
- A sprinkler in the backyard is still as much fun as you
  remember.
- Buy an annual family pass to the local zoo with unlimited
  visits. Instead of trying to see everything, choose one animal
  or continent per visit. Let the kids pick.
- Put on your bathing suits and wash the cars together.

Dad's

- "Watch your favorite guy flick (*Godfather, Terminator, Rocky,*
  et al.) every once in a while. You'll need it. Or introduce your
  favorite Jerry Lewis or Three Stooges to your kids, and all of
  you can have a laugh together. One hint, spare Mom the
  Stooges."
- One stay-at-home dad recommends pickup basketball at the
  local gym every Saturday. It's the perfect—and sweatiest—
  way to unwind.

Religious or Spiritual Training

- Make Sundays special. "It's tempting to sleep in on Sunday,
  worship St. Mattress as we affectionately call it, but then
  Sunday ends up being disjointed, full of chores and projects—just another day. When we go to church as a family we
  end up eating brunch together, then picking a family outing

like the park or zoo. The day becomes about being a family together. Errands? Never on Sunday."

- Keep your faith. "I'm the only dad dropping my son off at Hebrew school, but it's important to my wife and me that he understands his family's religion. We may have a nontraditional family structure, but we still honor our religious tradition."

Caring for Kids with Special Needs

- Don't isolate yourself or your child. "My son is disabled, so it's especially important for me to get out in the world and for him, too. The grocery store, the park, wherever. We just need that human contact."
- Get the support you need. One stay-at-home dad started a local public access television show about his daughter's condition. He had so many callers respond to his program that he formed a local support group—all while living out his dream of being on television.
- Remember that every kid loves to have fun. "At Halloween, we turn my son's wheelchair into a vehicle to match his costume. One year it was the Batmobile when he was Batman. Another year he was a cowboy with a covered wagon. The whole family helps construct it."

Basic Survival Techniques

- Take advantage of free delivery services: dry cleaners, pharmacy, groceries, meals . . . SAHDs need all the help they can get!
- Consider automatic bill-paying options. One less thing to deal with every month.
- Give up your ego. Surrender to the job. Submit and get over it.
- Change—that is, lower—your expectations. Life is different now and it always will be. Once you stop pining away for your old life, you'll be able to enjoy this new chapter of it.

- Get up. Get dressed. Get out.
- Don't make a long to-do list. It will only depress you. Instead, pick a couple of key things to do per day and do them.
- Go outside just for the sake of going outside.
- Stay connected to your pre-SAHD interests. "I got a subscription to the *Wall Street Journal* just to stay current. Someday I plan to return to the workforce, and this makes me feel like I'm still in the game."
- Beware of unwanted advice. It will come in droves. Be gracious, but consider the advice only if it's helpful. Ignore it if it's not.
- Learn to handle the lame queries of strangers. Find a pat answer that works for you. You'll definitely hear everyone's opinions about your choice to be a stay-at-home dad. Fuhgeddaboutit!
- Don't try to overdo, overschedule, or overload.

Maintaining Links to the Outside World

Make New Friends

- Make the most of the fact that everyone talks to you when you are carrying or pushing around a baby. (See above for personal hygiene, shaving, and clean clothing, so you don't scare away any potential friends.) You'll meet neighbors who never talked to you before. You'll meet other parents in the mall or at the grocery store. Salesclerks will actually assist you. You'll revel in the attention.
- Bring along single male friends on your daddy outings. They'll thank you for it when they discover that meeting women is easy when you have a baby with you.
- Go to a parent–baby Weight Watchers meeting. You'll meet moms and dads with common experiences.
- Develop relationships with women. (But don't get in trouble.) "At some point you'll talk like you're girlfriends. I now have the ability to relate as a human, not just as a man."

- Let strangers hold your baby occasionally. "I let more people hold the baby than my wife ever would. I guess I need that connection, and the baby provides a common link."

Keep the Old

- Hang out with some guys who aren't in touch with their feminine side. Your old buddies may not understand what you're doing. Don't try to make them, just forgive them and enjoy their company. It will be a nice break from the kids and house.
- Accept that your social circle will change a bit. Go with the friendship flow.

Things to Keep You Going and Energized

- "A smile from my daughter."
- "A snuggle from my baby boy."
- "When my little guy laughs at the silly things I do. I hear that big belly laugh coming from that little body and it makes me feel great."
- "When we sit down together at the dinner table and everyone starts talking all at once."
- "Every time someone says what a healthy, happy baby I have."
- "Every time I drive by the daycare facility."

Networking with Other Stay-at-Home Parents

- Join Gymboree or Music First classes with your baby. Check the "Y" or community centers for parent–child activities. Many have dad-based, or at least nonsexist, groups now.
- Go to the swings at the local park on a regular basis. You'll become familiar with the kids and parents and eventually make friends.
- Scouts, dance classes, music lessons, and sports are easy places to strike up conversations with other parents.
- Become a people person. "Men just aren't that good at net-

working. You have to try hard. It was pretty hard for me with number one, but by kid number two it was actually a lot of fun and I met a lot of nice people."

- Research the resources. There are great websites and support groups for SAHDs. Check out the Resource Guide in the Appendix to find some online support or a group in your area.

Creating Lasting Bonds with Other At-Home Dads

- Make a weekly SAHD date. "I meet another stay-at-home dad at the mall for coffee every Tuesday. The kids sit in the strollers and play with toys or nap while we discuss life. It's a critical part of making this work—feeling like you're not the only one doing it, comparing successes and failures. So what if we're the only dads in the mall on a Tuesday morning?"
- Find guys who understand the SAHD life—and support each other. "Both of our wives are doctors, so the two of us stay-at-home dads are in the same boat. We understand 'the life.' I'm in a jazz band that plays a couple gigs every month. I never know if my wife will be on call, so on performance nights I drop my daughter at my buddy's, and she sleeps in the trundle bed in his daughter's room. His two kids sleep over at our house in exchange when he and his wife want to go to dinner and the movies. You find people who understand you and back them up. I don't know a lot of stay-at-home moms that would have middle-of-the-week sleepovers, but for us dads it's a very cool thing."
- Check out Slowlane.com. It'll open up a wealth of SAHD wisdom.
- "Go to the At-Home Dad Convention every year. You'll be glad you did."

Resource Guide for SAHD/WM Families

Websites

www.Slowlane.com
www.Fathers First.org
www.Fatherhood.about.com
www.Daddyshome.com
www.DadMag.com
www.MrMomz.com
www.DadStaysHome.com

Newsletters/Periodicals

At-Home Dad Newsletter

61 Brightwood Avenue
North Andover, MA 01845-1702
AtHomeDad@aol.com

At-Home Dad Handbook

13925 Duluth Court
Apple Valley, MN 55124
DadtoDad@aol.com

Down to Earth Dad Newsletter

P.O. Box 1907
Coeur d'Alene, Idaho 83816
www.downtoearthdad.org
(877) 282-DADS [282-3237]

Fathering Magazine

www.fatheringmag.com

Full-Time Dads

www.fathersworld.com

Groups and Organizations

Dad-to-Dad

13925 Duluth Court
Apple Valley, MN 55124
DadtoDad@aol.com
www.slowlane.com/dad

Dads-at-Home (SAHD e-group)

www.groups.yahoo.com/group/dads-at-home

Cinncinnati Stay-at-Home Dads

www.members.tripod.com/cincidads/
cincinnatidads@cinci.rr.com

Families and Work Institute

212/465-2044
www.familiesandwork.org

Y-Indian Guides

www.indianguides.com

Girl Scouts of America

www.gsusa.org

Conventions/Conferences

At-Home Dads Convention

Oakton Community College
1600 Golf Road
Des Plaines, IL 60016
DrBobFrank@aol.com or www.Slowlane.com

Books

Raising Multiple Birth Children: A Parents' Survival Guide by
   William and Sheila Laut, along with Kristin Benit.
*Fatherneed: Why Father Care Is as Essential as Mother Care for Your
   Child* by Kyle D. Pruett, M.D.
*Parenting Partners: How to Encourage Dads to Participate in the
   Daily Lives of Their Children* by Robert Frank, Ph.D., with
   Kathryn E. Livingston.

Being There: The Benefits of a Stay-at-Home Parent by Isabelle Fox, Ph.D., with Norman M. Lobsenz.

If You Can't Make Time, Don't Make Children by Steve Smith.

You Can Afford to Stay Home with Your Kids by Malia McCawley Wyckoff and Mary Snyder.

How Can I Ever Afford To Have Children? Money Skills for New and Experienced Parents by Barbara Hetzer.

A Father's Love, A Daughter's Power by Richard Axel.

Father Courage: What Happens When Men Put Family First by Suzanne Braun Levine.

How to Talk So Kids Will Listen, and Listen So Kids Will Talk by Adele Faber, Elaine Mazlish, and Kimberly Ann Coe.

Raising Cain: Protecting the Emotional Life of Boys by Daniel J. Kindlon, Michael Thompson, Dan Kindlon, and Teresa Barker.

Don't Make Me Stop This Car: Adventures in Fatherhood by Al Roker.

The Barefoot Book of Father and Son Tales by Josephine Evetts-Secker and Helen Cann.

Acknowledgments

I am grateful to the many people who helped shape this book: first of all, to my family for their incredible patience and support. But mostly to Ned, who lived this book every day as a loving full-time parent to our two boys, while I was a working mom who also managed to pursue a dream.

I am indebted to Harvey Klinger for taking a chance on a new writer and a new concept, as well as everyone at Plume for shepherding me through my maiden literary experience, particularly Amanda Patten and Brant Janeway. No one could ask for a better team!

And, of course, I could never have written this book without the generosity of an amazing community of stay-at-home dads, their working wives, and their children, who willingly contributed personal stories, parenting tips, and resources. I am beyond grateful to Slowlane.com's Jay Massey, a tireless source of wit, wisdom, and insight. A special thanks also to Joann Massey, Bob Frank, Jim and Leslie DiCenzo, Bill and Sheila Laut, Hogan and Tina Hilling, Barry and Lori Reszel, Casey Spencer, Chris Coby, Mitch Silver, and Brian Lowry.

To Nancy LeVine, David Fox, and Andy Kaplan: I can't thank you enough for your invaluable personal and professional guidance. I continue to be awed by the talent, kindness, and care of my incredible note-giving friends, Laura Golden Bellotti, Nancy Joslin Kaleel, and Nancy Oliver. My thanks to Michael Illig, Michelle Hair-Foti, and Terrance Meyer for their financial expertise and input. And to my literary brother, Cameron Chambers, for his constant encouragement.

And finally, my thanks to many gracious friends and colleagues for their support and faith, especially John Kalish, Suzy Unger, John Ferriter, Mark Itkin, Scott Sternberg, Gara Rakow, Phil Gurin, Sharon Williams, Bridgett Walther, Laura Galloway, Erik Thompson, Sheila Feren, Pam Golum, Alison Lazar, Ferdie Pacheco, Lonnie Burstein, Valerie Schaer, Elizabeth Herbst, and all my former associates at Studios USA.

Index